Following Jesus

Following Jesus

In an Age of Hypocrisy

DAVID LOWRY

WIPF & STOCK · Eugene, Oregon

FOLLOWING JESUS
In an Age of Hypocrisy

Copyright © 2020 David Lowry. All rights reserved. Except for brief quotations in critical publications or reviews, no part of this book may be reproduced in any manner without prior written permission from the publisher. Write: Permissions, Wipf and Stock Publishers, 199 W. 8th Ave., Suite 3, Eugene, OR 97401.

The Scripture quotations contained herein are from the New Revised Standard Version of the Bible, copyrighted 1989, by the Division of Christian Education of the National Council of Churches of Christ in the U.S.A. Used by permission. All rights reserved.

Scripture quotations noted CEB are taken from the Common English Bible, copyright 2011. Used by permission. All rights reserved.

Wipf & Stock
An Imprint of Wipf and Stock Publishers
199 W. 8th Ave., Suite 3
Eugene, OR 97401

www.wipfandstock.com

PAPERBACK ISBN: 978-1-7252-6381-9
HARDCOVER ISBN: 978-1-7252-6377-2
EBOOK ISBN: 978-1-7252-6380-2

Manufactured in the U.S.A. 04/22/20

Contents

Introduction		vii
1	The Desire to Follow	1
2	The Decision to Follow	14
3	The Act of Following	21
4	The Identity of the Follower	32
5	Following Love	44
6	The Gathering of Followers	61
7	Following the Crucified and Risen One	73
8	Witness in An Age of Hypocrisy	90
Bibliography		113

Introduction

In this soul-weary world, a human being came and said to other human beings, "Come to me, all you that are weary and are carrying heavy burdens, and I will give you rest. Take my yoke upon you, and learn from me; for I am gentle and humble in heart, and you will find rest for your souls."[1] It was an unusual message for one human being to declare to others—offering rest for their souls. It spoke to a deep human need. And people came!

For those weary of lies, Jesus spoke truth. For those weary with burdens—theirs and others—Jesus offered rest. To the brokenhearted, he offered comfort. To the sick, he offered healing. To those bound, he offered liberation. To the guilt-ridden, he offered forgiveness. To many, he offered a fresh start and a new life. He offered himself. He served others with compassion. He loved. Both his words and his life brought light. And he viewed his death as a dying for the liberation of many.

Jesus' life and words remain an attraction. Through the writings of the New Testament, we are invited to receive from him what he offers. And his life and teaching continue to speak to us, as they have in every age. Furthermore, through the witness of the Gospels, we are invited to follow him. The New Testament assumes that anyone of any time and place can become a follower. Jesus is lifted up as crucified and risen, "the same yesterday and today and forever," present and available to all.[2] Through the witness of his first followers, Jesus' words touch our deepest desire, the desire for God, for the source of our lives. Not only his words, but what is testified of his life, draw us. Jesus clearly lives in deep communion with God. The way he operates with authority, his centered sense of identity and his profound compassion attract us to his life. Here is a human being who knows who he is and what he comes to do. And he does it powerfully. We are drawn toward him. Above all, his love astounds us and we desire it.

1. Matt 11:28–29.
2. Heb 13:8.

Behind Paul's descriptions of love is Jesus' kind of love, love that is genuine, responds to the needs of others, shows hospitality to strangers, prays for those who persecute us, "rejoices with those who rejoice and weeps with those who weep," "associates with the lowly," feeds enemies when they are hungry and provides water when they thirst.[3] It can be said of this love embodied in Jesus: "Love is patient; love is kind; love is not envious or boastful or arrogant or rude. It does not insist on its own way; it is not irritable or resentful; it does not rejoice in wrongdoing, but rejoices in the truth. It bears all things, believes all things, hopes all things, endures all things."[4] This love rescues, frees, and heals us.

Whenever this love is encountered, we are drawn to it. We desire it. It may draw us near to Jesus, as so many others have been before us. Desire is where we all start. It is where this book starts. Desire moves us to the point of decision and with decision, the first steps of following. It is in the daily act of following that we gain our identity as "participants of the divine nature" and then find ourselves united with others who have entered this same reality.[5]

As the witness of the New Testament indicates, Jesus always leads us to "the Father" and to the reign of God in which we find our true home. When God reigns in our hearts—for whom our hearts are made—other usurpers are dethroned. We are set free to be our true selves as received from the source of our lives. We become witnesses, not only as individuals, but as communities, to the ways of God's reign and government. Our witness runs counter to the prevailing ways of the world and its governments.

The Gospel of John summarizes this reality with the words of Jesus to Pilate, "My kingdom is not from this world. If my kingdom were from this world, my followers would be fighting to keep me from being handed over to the Jews [Judean authorities]. But as it is, my kingdom is not from here." Then Jesus makes clear the purpose of his life, "For this I was born, and for this I came into the world, to testify to the truth." In a world of lies and deceit, Jesus testifies to the truth. In a world of darkness, Jesus is the light. As if anticipating our attempts to fit Jesus to our false selves rather than be fitted to him, Jesus says, "Everyone who belongs to the truth listens to *my* voice."[6]

Among the many voices present in our lives, within and without, there is the voice of Christ: that is, the voice of truth that guides us into our true selves. Whatever it is that we may be enduring, whatever the trials, whatever the state of our inner life with its various emotions and attitudes, there is a

3. Rom 12:9–21.
4. 1 Cor 12:4–7.
5. 2 Pet 1:4.
6. John 18:33–38.

voice that leads us into reality. Our feelings often describe what we are going through, but generally do not tell us *what* to do; that is, they do not direct us into our genuine humanity. Nor do the many ideologies that we create to secure our false allegiances and false selves do so. We must hear the "still small voice" that leads us into life. We recognize that voice in Jesus, who speaks truth and calls us back to the source of our lives.

While this book is about following Jesus as a way into God's presence and purposes, I expect that those who come from other religious traditions will find points of correspondence when it comes to human spiritual experience as described here. After all, human beings have found many ways to express their experience of the "nameless one." Experiences of surrender, of relinquishing our lives, of being centered, of love and compassion, faith, and grace have found many forms. The Christian notion of incarnation has to do with God's availability to all humankind. God's self-expression has become flesh, God joined to our humanity so that our true humanity is only found in union with God, which is available to all. Whatever our faith tradition, we can become alienated from its essential reality. Those who go by the name of Christ can end up with the accouterments of a tradition, having lost its center. We can even end up with a religious ideology that binds and demeans us and others.

Our age needs followers of Jesus, for whom Christ is not a doctrinal abstraction but a living and trusted person whose leading receives the response of obedience to the truth. As with every age, evil is an ever present constant. Education, "high culture," and "exceptionalism" do not prevent wars, genocides, atom bombs being created and used, poverty, and oppression. There is always a need for clear witness to an alternate way of life. Jesus, who proclaimed God's way and governance, offers to the world the alternative which is life centered in God. Those who have come into this life are witnesses to it.

The problem is that not all who put themselves forward as witnesses, who claim the name of Christ, are followers of Jesus. They may participate in a church culture and a form of religion, but their roots are in the "spirit of the world." They live far removed from the kind of community Jesus gathers around himself and they are alienated from the "Spirit that is from God."[7] Christian language, for them, becomes a cover for false allegiances, including commitments to nation and race.

The title of this book is *Following Jesus: In an Age of Hypocrisy*, with special regard for religious hypocrisy. Of course, every age has its hypocrisies. We have ours: a prosperity gospel seemingly made for TV and marketing, a

---

7. 1 Cor 2:12.

legalistic and judgmental religion that is far from Jesus who said he did not come into the world to condemn, a fundamentalist and biblicist religion that is closed to science and to the many various ways truth comes to us, and a kind of sentimentalist Christianity that is simply "nice" and avoids truly challenging people.

Along with these examples, and that which has made many feel acutely the present religious hypocrisy, is the recent support for Donald Trump by a large majority of self-identified evangelicals. We have heard evangelical leaders rationalize their support in the most extraordinary ways, some speaking of Trump in glowing terms and others announcing that God had ordained him to the office of the presidency. Whatever witness these leaders may have had to Jesus formerly has virtually vanished before the world. And what American evangelicalism had previously represented, it did no more—at least in the witness of these leaders. It was as if it had gained the world politically and lost its soul. There are, of course, evangelicals who have provided a countering witness, but they appear to be a minority.

Add to the above hypocrisies the state of historic mainline Protestant churches, who, while providing some degree of moral witness and care for justice, often offer little in the way of spiritual vitality. And the Roman Catholic Church, while demonstrating care for social justice and the needy, nevertheless has been rocked by issues of sexual abuse among clergy. At times, it seems, we have to look beyond the formal organized church to find witnesses to Jesus' teaching and way of life.

Where we do see witnesses among those who go by the name of Christ, it is because there is a simple following of Jesus. The answer to Christian hypocrisy is faithful obedience to the call and word of Christ. Where there are *communities* of followers who are learning faithful obedience to the truth in the power of the Spirit, we see corporate manifestations of doing justice, loving mercy, and walking humbly before God. From such communities the good news that Christ offers to the world is going forth concretely in word and action. These faithful communities show up among historic mainline churches, nondenominational churches, house churches, monastic communities, newly formed gatherings committed to a spiritual journey, and ecumenical communities.

While the subtitle of this book is "In an Age of Hypocrisy," the issue of hypocrisy forms only a part of the background of this book and not the central aspect. The nearer background is our humanity and the human condition. The foreground is simply the nature and dynamic of following Jesus. It is the reality of following Jesus that strips away hypocrisy and addresses our deepest desire, which is for God, the source of our being.

1

The Desire to Follow

"As a deer longs for flowing streams so my soul longs for you, O God."

PSALM 42:1

Why did Peter and Andrew, James and John, Mary Magdalene, Joanna, Salome, and the other disciples *want* to follow Jesus? What was there about Jesus that drew them to him, that brought forth a *desire* to follow and kept them following?

Jesus did not promise them prosperity, certainly not along the lines of made-for-TV prosperity preachers. He did not place wealth, health, and wisdom at the center of his teaching, nor did he live what we generally consider a prosperous lifestyle. Like John the Baptist, Jesus did not hang around the wealthy and powerful. After John's death, Jesus asked those who came out to see John, "What did you go out into the wilderness to look at?" Did you go to see "someone dressed in soft robes? Look, those who wear soft robes are in royal palaces."

Like John, Jesus was not found in centers of power but out in the wilderness or going from town to town. When we consider the names of the towns that Jesus visited, they were small. Nazareth, his home town was small. Maybe two hundred people lived there.[1] During the years of his ministry, he made his home in Capernaum, another small town, on the shores of Galilee. Capernaum was only ten miles from Tiberias, the capital city

---

1. Lizorkin-Eyzenberg, *The Jewish Gospel of John*, 18.

of Galilee, where King Herod Antipas had his royal palace, but there is no mention of Jesus going there. He did not cozy up to power. He did not attempt to get close to King Herod or to the world's powerful, as if they had something to offer him. Jesus came with his own authority and power, as one who had something to give—giving from what he was daily receiving. So he was often with needy people, who knew they were needy: the blind, the lame, the brokenhearted, the emotionally and mentally ill.

The only time we read of Jesus going to a major city, a place of power and prestige, was when he went to Jerusalem. There he confronted and called out the Judean leadership. Chapter 23 of Matthew gives us a sense of the threat he posed to the political order, given what he said to them. ("Woe to you hypocrites." "Woe to you blind guides." "You are like whitewashed tombs, which on the outside look beautiful, but inside they are full of the bones of the dead and of all kinds of filth.") He was brought by angry leaders to stand before King Herod and then Pilate, the Roman governor, to whom he was presented as a danger to Rome, with the accusation that he was a treacherous usurper who made himself out to be king of the Jews. As he had prophesied to his disciples, he was then executed, dying the death of a subversive.

So, why did these disciples want to follow Jesus? What did they desire? There were those, at that time, who anticipated the redemption of Israel and associated the liberation of their nation with an anointed one (a messiah[2]), a son of David. There were those who imagined the reestablishing of the kingdom that God promised to David and his descendants. They looked for Mount Zion, upon which sat the temple, to be lifted up as the highest of the mountains to which all the nations of the world would come and worship the God of Israel and all creation.[3] But in the disciples' initial encounter with Jesus, that scenario was likely more than they could have envisioned, except as a hopeful possibility.[4] At the least, they initially saw in Jesus a teacher, prophet, and healer.

Before Jesus came to Peter, James, and John on the shores of the Sea of Galilee and called them to follow him, they must have had some experience with Jesus. Jesus had made his home in Capernaum on the Sea of Galilee and he ministered in that area, sometimes in the town, sometimes out in

---

2. "Messiah," "Christ," and "Anointed One" are used interchangeably, as a title for Jesus, in this book. "Messiah" (Hebrew) and "Christos" (Greek) are translated "Anointed."

3. Isa 2:2; Mic 4:1.

4. The Gospel of John has this hope articulated by Andrew to his brother Simon, "We have found the Messiah " (John 1:41). In the Synoptic Gospels (Matt, Mark, Luke) the confession of Jesus as Messiah comes later after the disciples have spent considerable time with Jesus.

deserted places, sometimes in his home. We are also given the impression, in Matthew and Luke, that Peter's house was in Capernaum.[5] And Luke implies that Jesus had a relationship with Simon Peter prior to calling him. Jesus was in Peter's house, healing his mother-in-law, prior to telling him that "from now on you will be catching people," and prior to Peter leaving everything to follow him.[6] Peter and his companions heard Jesus speak and saw him heal before they received the call to follow. Above all, they heard Jesus proclaim the nearness of God's reign and call people to make themselves ready to receive God's reign.

Clearly, Jesus' message concerning God's reign was central to his identity. So, how did Jesus' followers understand the proclamation that the kingdom of God had come near? They likely understood God's kingdom in earthly terms, that Israel would be free from the occupation of Rome, that the temple on Mount Zion would be filled with God's presence, and that Israel would become a light to all nations. After all, James and John at one point desired to be made second to Jesus when he came into his kingdom—revealing a politically typical view of the nature of kingdoms. That the kingdom was near, that the waiting was almost over, that the kingdom was neither far in time or space must have brought great hope, no matter whatever way they envisioned God's kingdom. That God reigns, of course, was in keeping with what they knew of God from their Scriptures as the source and center of all, the ruler of all, the one we are to love with our whole being, serve, trust, and obey.[7]

However they may have initially understood God's reign, what we see in these potential followers was a desire for God's presence and action in their lives and the lives of their people. They wanted God to reign. They desired a world where God had dominion instead of evil, instead of Satan.

---

5. In Matthew, after healing a centurion's servant in Capernaum, Jesus enters Peter's house (Matt 8:14). In Luke, after casting out an unclean demon from a man in the synagogue in Capernaum, Jesus enters Peter's house and heals his mother-in-law (Luke 4:31–39). In John, however, we are told that Andrew and his brother, Peter, are from Bethsaida (John 1:43). Of course, it may be that Bethsaida was Peter's hometown in the same way Nazareth was Jesus' hometown. Both Bethsaida and Capernaum were at the northern end of the Sea of Galilee.

6. Luke 5:10–11.

7. Representative of passages lifting up God's kingdom or dominion are these verses from two psalms. Ps 22:27–28: "All the ends of the earth shall remember / and turn to the Lord; / and all the families of the nations / shall worship before him. /For dominion belongs to the Lord, / and he rules over the nations." Ps 145:10–13: "All your works shall give thanks to you, O Lord, / and all your faithful shall bless you. / They shall speak of the glory of your kingdom, / and tell of your power, / to make known to all people your mighty deeds, / and the glorious splendor of your kingdom. / Your kingdom is an everlasting kingdom, / and your dominion endures throughout all generations."

They desired the life they saw in Jesus: the compassion, the truth, the authority over evil and disease. God was powerfully present in Jesus, and they desired that presence. They encountered, in Jesus, powerful compassion, mercy, and truth. God's will was being done through Jesus. It was something beautiful to behold, and they wanted to be included in that reality.

They desired to follow Jesus because, in the words of the Gospel of John, he had "the words of eternal life."[8] They wanted what he had. They needed what he had to give. They saw the intimacy that he had with God; he called God "father." They saw the way Jesus prayed and its importance in his life, and they asked him to teach them how to pray. They desired the kind of relationship Jesus had with God. That is still why potential followers come to have a desire to follow Jesus.

It was not Jesus' politics, principles, or ethical stance that attracted them. It was God. It was about getting near to someone who experiences God, who exercises authority that comes from God, and who operates by the power of God to bring healing and liberation. Theirs was the most fundamental human desire, to be one with the source of their lives and live from that reality and to experience that reality in the world.

Many of us, who have been exposed to Jesus through church confessions, creedal formulas, and rituals, have had to take a fresh look at Jesus, doing what the first disciples did: taking steps to get to know him. We have had to take one step after another. Without such steps, we were in danger of subscribing to creeds that we did not understand or held little meaning for us. It may even have been that our religious culture and its beliefs had moved away from the reality of Jesus.

Peter, James, and John, and Mary Magdalene and Joanna, did not start following Jesus because they believed he was God, but because Jesus, a human being like them, manifested a particular kind of life that was attractive to them. In response to that attraction, they began to take steps of receiving and then understanding. They only came to recognize Jesus as divine through his humanity. It is the only way any of us come to "see" God. God comes to us through our humanity. (That is what Christians have meant by "incarnation.")

Whether we have been "indoctrinated" into a Christian belief system or have been distant from that experience, makes no difference. We all have to take the kind of steps these first followers took. We start with a desire for something we encounter in the words and life of Jesus, or the words and life of someone who has experience with God. We may wonder, as these first followers of Jesus did, how it was that he or someone in our lives addresses

---

8. John 6:68.

God in intimate, personal terms, like, "dear Father." Jesus' first followers heard him pray in this way and they wanted to know how they should pray. He told them to pray, "dear Father." This intimate relationship was for them as well.

What Jesus' life and words touch in us is a fundamental desire for God. Not for *a* god, or a supreme being, or a supernatural being. We can imagine for ourselves a being above us, higher than us, to whom we might appeal when things are not working out and, who when called upon, will work in our favor, as we imagine that favor to be. Our deepest desire, however, is not for such a being: a being among other beings, the highest of them all who when called upon can do our bidding. Our desire transcends all such definable beings and finite desires. It is a desire for the *source* of our lives, for the one we cannot name, one who fits none of our categories, one who, in the words of theologian, Karl Rahner, is "incomprehensible mystery."[9] We desire the One from whom we and all things come into being and in whom we find our being. We desire the One from whom all love, beauty, and life flows.

In the words of the Genesis story of creation, we were "created in God's image after God's likeness." We are that creature who has God stamped upon us. We are fitted for experiencing God. We have an infinite openness which reaches beyond all finite realities, for the One from whom all things come. In all our knowing of our world and of one another, there is an implicit reaching out to God. In all our loving, there is an underlying desire for God. As Jesus makes clear, when we love our neighbor, we are at the same time loving God. And we cannot love God and not love our neighbor. We are imprinted with God, and we desire God in our inmost hearts.

We desire the kind of life that comes from the God who is love and who welcomes all. When we encounter a life, a human being, who expresses that love, we desire it with the fundamental desire we have for knowing God. We see in the first followers of Jesus their attraction to the way Jesus operated. He acted as one who lives from his source. He stands out as "not of this world," not of a world turned inward and closed in upon itself in the idolatry of self. We see, in Jesus, one who is open to God and others in love.

Jesus' disciples noticed that Jesus exercised a different kind of authority from that which they had experienced from other teachers.[10] His authority was recognized both in his teaching and in his commands that delivered individuals from the power of evil and brought healing.[11] Jesus operated

---

9. Karl Rahner uses this phrase in many places among his writings. See, for example, his chapter on "Man in the Presence of Absolute Mystery" in Rahner, *Foundations*, 44–51.

10. Mark 1:22.

11. Luke 4:32–41.

with power. Jesus lived from the center. The source of his authority and power was God.

Jesus' life was centered in the manner expressed by the central commandment of the Hebrew Scriptures, which was "You shall love the Lord your God with all your heart, and with all your soul, and with all your mind."[12] Jesus lived the essence of that command. And he recognized that there was a second like it: "You shall love your neighbor as yourself."[13] Jesus taught that every commandment of God, as well as our ability to discern what God commands, flows from loving God with our whole selves.

His first followers saw that love of God concretely. They saw it in the way Jesus reached out with compassion and mercy. "When he saw the crowds, he had compassion for them, because they were harassed and helpless, like sheep without a shepherd."[14] "When he went ashore, he saw a great crowd; and he had compassion for them and cured their sick."[15] He spoke up for those who were oppressed. Of unjust leaders, he said, "They tie up heavy burdens, hard to bear, and lay them on the shoulders of others; but they themselves are unwilling to lift a finger to move them."[16] He loved in a way that spoke hard truth to those in power and to all who sought a center from which to live other than God. Above all, Jesus called people back to God, the source of their lives and relationships. Finally, he gave his life as a "ransom for many."[17] Jesus viewed his death as a liberating act. He gave his life in obedience to God's call and for the sake of the world.

Jesus' words and actions of mercy and compassion were attractive to those who desired after the God who is love. Our deepest desire is for unconditional love and wholeness. That desire can also be described as our fundamental need. We need God. We cannot live without God or be, on our own, the true selves that God created us to be. Our very identity comes from God. And yet we have tried to construct our lives without God. We have constructed and operated from false selves. Consequently, we are in need of liberation, from bondage to that which takes away our being and empties us of reality.

We need one who comes to liberate. We need the Jesus of the Gospel of John: "If the Son makes you free, you will be free indeed."[18] When the New

---

12. Deut 6:5; Mark 12:29–30; Matt 22:37; Luke 10:27.
13. Matt 22:37–39.
14. Matt 9:36.
15. Matt 14:14.
16. Matt 23:4.
17. Matt 20:28; Mark 10:45.
18. John 8:36.

Testament speaks of salvation, it is about rescue, liberation, and healing. In the pages of the four Gospels, we see Jesus on a rescue mission of delivering people who are bound by disease, evil, and oppression. In the Gospel of John, Jesus says, "I came that they may have life, and have it abundantly."[19] In the Synoptic Gospels, it is, "I have come to seek and to save (heal and deliver) the lost."[20] People were attracted to Jesus' mission to liberate. Those who chose to follow him desired to be engaged in that same work of rescuing and liberating.

DESIRE FOR LIBERATION AND A LIBERATOR

I choose the word *liberator* over *savior* because it better captures the meaning of Jesus' life and vocation for our time. *Savior* has come to be a religious word related, in the minds of many, to salvation from sins, and often narrowly signifies God's forgiveness and acceptance. Notwithstanding the importance of forgiveness and acceptance, the liberating work of God expressed in Jesus' ministry is broad. It encompasses healing from disease, deliverance from evil powers, liberation from oppression, transformation and union with God.

In many congregations, Christians have learned to confess that "we are captive to sin and cannot free ourselves."[21] With these words, we express our foundational need for liberation. We confess the nature of our condition. Our problem is not primarily one of "sins," but "sin" as a state of bondage. It is a condition of being turned in upon ourselves, attempting to make ourselves the center of our own lives and, as well, our inability to free ourselves. We are in need of God's grace. That is, we are in need of liberation as a gift. We need *God* to liberate us. That God comes to liberate us means we are forgiven as well. The good news of the New Testament is that God has rescued and delivered us through Jesus as the Christ (the "Anointed One"). "In Christ God was reconciling the world to himself, not counting their trespasses against them."[22]

Our need is for liberation. When we begin to break out of the denial of our mortality and creatureliness, when we acknowledge that we are not ultimately in control and can never be the center of our existence, then we

---

19. John 10:10.

20. "Synoptic" has the sense of "similar point of view," and refers to the gospels of Matt, Mark, and Luke. The Greek word for save (sozo) has the sense of rescue, heal, and deliver.

21. Evangelical Lutheran Church in America, *Lutheran Worship*, 95.

22. 2 Cor 5:19.

begin to realize our need for liberation. We find we are quite incapable of liberating ourselves. We are unable to stop playing at being our own creators. We have great difficulty giving up control. We do, indeed, have things under our control, but we take on far more than fits the reality of our being creatures subject to death. When we begin to come out of denial, we begin to recognize that we have been running from our mortality. The love of "super-heroes" is a conspicuous example. But the way we use religion is another.

We replace God's liberating work, the liberation we truly need, with a salvation from death in the form of a future "everlasting life," while, at the same time, leaving largely untouched our present condition. As such, religion is used as a cover for our mortality problem, so that, rather than learning from our mortality, rather than receiving the gift that is present when we truly accept our mortality and vulnerability and creatureliness, we go on living as if we can construct our lives from the false center of ourselves. We go on living as if we could replace God. Religion serves our bondage to this false centering.

This underlying spiritual dysfunction manifests itself in what St. Paul calls the flesh: our disoriented desires and values, our loss of love, our inhumanity, our unjust treatment of others, our lack of mercy, our judgmentalism, our prejudices, and our oppressive ways. It shows itself in the breakdown of our relationships, our societies, and the world. It is seen in the divisions we have constructed of race, class, and gender. Further, it has a bearing on mental illness and all manner of dis-ease. We need liberation on many levels: body, soul, and spirit; relational and societal; national and global.

We have a fundamental desire for liberation and a liberator. Our experience has demonstrated that we cannot free ourselves, whether as individuals, communities, or nations. We feel the need for rescue and we desire liberation, but we are like those who struggle with drug addiction whose wills have become bent around their drug habit. We cannot free ourselves from trying to be our own centers. We need outside help. Saint Paul wrote of the experience of captivity to the in-turned, egocentric life that causes so much heartache. And then writes, "Wretched man that I am! Who will rescue me?" His answer? "Thanks be to God through Jesus Christ our Lord!"[23] Our deepest desire for God is also a desire for God to set us free.

However, the desire for a liberator, high-jacked by the idolatry of self, has spawned many false liberators, from authoritarians to guru-type individuals. It should not surprise us that we latch onto false liberators and

---

23. Rom 7:21–25.

ideologies. It is another expression of our bondage. We cannot free ourselves from this spiritual bondage. When we attempt to fix what we perceive as our problem, we choose as our leaders those who operate in the same cycle of bondage, and from ideologies that only add to our destruction. Our breaking free is not accomplished by our own resources apart from God. We have to cooperate with what God comes to do. It is God who is our liberator. What is true for us was true for the first followers of Jesus. They desired God as the source and center of their lives and as the one who liberates them from all that would keep them from their true center. That they came to see, in Jesus, God's presence and action, had to do with both what was manifest in his life and the contextual signs that were elements in Israel's history. Their desire for God and God's rescue was grounded historically in messianic expectations; and yet, fundamentally, that desire is a human desire we all share. It is there in all histories and societies, but that desire is not necessarily recognized.

ATTRACTED, CONFLICTED, AND OFFENDED

Jesus' words and actions both attracted and repulsed. Some came needy for what Jesus offered. Others were offended by Jesus' words and actions. I read Matthew, chapter 23, to Bible students. It is a long discourse in which Jesus declares a message of judgment against leaders, with such words as:

> Woe to you, scribes and Pharisees, hypocrites! For you lock people out of the kingdom of heaven. For you do not go in yourselves, and when others are going in, you stop them. Woe to you, scribes and Pharisees, hypocrites! For you cross sea and land to make a single convert, and you make the new convert twice as much a child of hell as yourselves. . . .
> Woe to you, scribes and Pharisees, hypocrites! For you are like whitewashed tombs, which on the outside look beautiful, but inside they are full of the bones of the dead and of all kinds of filth. So you also on the outside look righteous to others, but inside you are full of hypocrisy and lawlessness.[24]

At the end of reading this chapter to the class, one of the students blurted out, "He had to go!" It was clear, in the way our world operates, that those in positions of authority, to whom Jesus was addressing these words, would have to get rid of him, as their ancestors did with the prophets before him. Jesus says as much when he calls them the "descendants of those who

---

24. Matt 23:13–15, 27–28.

murdered the prophets." The source of their authority put them in opposition to prophets. Jesus also understood what this meant for himself, personally.

Today, those who are called to declare a "word of the Lord" must expect to offend. If the word we speak never brings offense, it is not the word of God. "Woe to you when all speak well of you, for that is what their ancestors did to the false prophets."[25]

Not all were offended by Jesus' words in such a manner as wanting to deprive him of life. Some simply could not remain listening to words that called forth change that would disturb and unsettle their lives as they had constructed them. "Because of this [Jesus' difficult teaching] many of his disciples turned back and no longer went about with him. So Jesus asked the twelve, 'Do you also wish to go away?' Simon Peter answered him, 'Lord, to whom can we go? You have the words of eternal life.'"[26]

Apparently, the "words of eternal life" are hard truth and challenge us to turn and receive a radically new life. Some are offended by the warnings of judgment; others, by the radical call to new life and to our true selves. Our deepest desire is for God, but, since that desire has been in captivity, the call back to God meets resistance. Our will is divided and there is a struggle. It is God who liberates, but God awaits our "yes" to God's liberation.

It is difficult to encounter Jesus' life in the witness of the Gospels and to hear his words and to not experience a radical call. If we are gaining ears to hear (and our deep desire for God helps us here), we eventually find ourselves confronted with a decision that has to do with the whole of our lives. Our desire helps us into a search, a striving after God's reign and presence. We need to take up this search. Jesus encourages us to do so: "Ask, and it will be given you; search, and you will find; knock, and the door will be opened for you. For everyone who asks receives, and everyone who searches finds, and for everyone who knocks, the door will be opened."[27] Our desire helps us into a search and the search brings us to the point of decision.

THE CREATURE WHO SEEKS

We are seekers, every one of us. It is inescapable. We all do it, and we do it all the time. We are always looking for something, knocking at some door, seeking for some new experience, reaching out for something more than

---

25. Luke 6:26.
26. John 6:66–68.
27. Matt 7:7–8.

what we presently know or have. In all that we do, we seek, we question, we wonder.

Not only do we seek, but there is no end to our seeking. We have an immense appetite for more, always more. Some of us who live in an affluent society, and who have "benefited" materially from that society, demonstrate this by our collection of *things*. There are those who can open a closet and see more pieces of clothing than can be worn in a year. Such accumulation is not based on any real need for covering, but rather mirrors an unfathomable search for something more. There is never enough. We approach life with an unbounded desire, an infinite reaching out, always seeking. Enough is not "enough" even when it is all or more than we need. The experience which is mine right now is not enough; I want more experiences, more power, more knowledge, more information; more, more, more. It is not difficult for many of us to see that much of our seeking is misplaced (although we may not know how it got misplaced). We may name our tendency toward over-accumulation as "greed," but greed is only misplaced desire. Before there is greed, there is a human seeking, which is boundless. Whether our seeking is misplaced or not, it is open-ended; it is infinitely open-ended. There is no end to our seeking.

I asked a young man what he wanted in life. He had tried sex, drugs, and Jesus and was ready to go on to something else, not having been satisfied. His answer to my question was, "I just want to be happy." It is probably the most prevalent answer to the question of what we are all seeking. In these United States of America, it tends to be a self-evident truth. But it is not true that we are ultimately seeking happiness in all that we do.

When our seeking is true to our most basic desire, it is a seeking after *being*. Many years ago I watched my four-year-old daughter in the yard and wrote down what I saw:

> She has been playing with several puppies for hours. Her whole being expresses delight. It is the joy of life I see in her. It is well-being, rooted in being. It is life she is taking in as she walks barefoot in the grass, lies down, letting a puppy get tangled in her hair. Her happiness is the happiness of being, of being alive, of being enraptured by life, by a life other than her own. The life of the puppy enters into her being and she is taken by the mystery of its reality.

It was being; it was the truth of this wonderful puppy creature that was the cause of my daughter's happiness. It was not happiness she was seeking, but life. She quite naturally was seeking because it was her nature to do so. She sought what *is*, and happiness followed. This is a simple, basic truth, and the violation of it is the fundamental cause of our discontentment. If we would lose ourselves to the *real*, to *being itself*, we would find ourselves.

We seek our true selves. We seek being or life that is truly appropriate to whom we are becoming. We seek that reality that is us, which is our true coming-to-be. After all, we do not come into the world already having in our possession the reality we will become. We have the bare beginnings of a self that is in the process of becoming. Our self does not hold its life within it, but must go outside itself for the gift of its life. Therefore we continually stretch out for more of life. We are always on the way to becoming more than we presently are, stretching out for the fuller realization of our true selves.

When I say that we seek our true selves, I do not mean we seek our true selves in and of ourselves, as if the truth of our being were to be found in ourselves by ourselves. Rather, our seeking is an infinite reaching out and is only satisfied by infinite being. We become who we truly are only by finding ourselves in the boundless and "nameless" One, the source of our lives. So, when Jesus says, "Search and you will find," he is speaking to this foundational human reality: our hunger for God. This hunger and seeking is not content with any particular reality, but reaches out for God.

When we make a particular reality, a creaturely reality, that which we seek and live for with ultimacy, then our seeking is misplaced and that particular reality is an idol. We "exchange the truth about God for a lie and worship and serve the creature rather than the Creator, who is blessed forever!"[28] Our spiritual hunger has become turned in upon ourselves. We seek to make ourselves the center from which to live. We seek to make our selves that reality from which we find ourselves. We attempt that which is impossible, for we are not the center. We are not that from which all that exists comes. In our attempt to be our own center, we lose ourselves. We become unreal. The self we seemingly grow is a false self and the truth is far from us.

If I seek to live life on my own terms, I really end up living life on somebody or something else's terms. I live for my job or my nation or an ideology or some "great cause." I live for my pleasure (a very small cause). I live for my happiness; I seek knowledge, not for truth, but for information and its potential for positioning myself. Thus I am manipulated by the very information I seek to use to manipulate others. My manipulating others becomes my identity. The information I use is not knowledge—certainly not knowledge of myself, which is the knowledge I most need. This information has no value for my becoming. It is, rather, the means by which I distinguish myself from and maintain power over others. I have done what society has

---

28. Rom 1:25.

indicated I must do to become somebody, but in fact I have lost myself. I am nothing more than a sad creature groping to be what I cannot be. No matter how much I attempt to lord it over others, I cannot be a god. I am just another manipulator who is the object of others' manipulations.

The essential struggle of our lives is with whether or not we will let God, from whom all being flows, be the source of our lives. We have an infinite searching hunger, because it is the infinite, unbounded God that we seek. We cannot know our true selves except through knowing God. Our true selves are a gift from God, from whom all that is real comes. Because we come to God already committed to false selves, we must undergo conversion, the turning from a false self to our true self, the turning from the attempt to find our self within our self to finding our self in God. All of life is to be a conversion. Every day is to be a turning to God. We are, in the words of the old Shaker song, to "turn, turn, until by turning we come 'round right."

Therefore, Jesus says, "Repent for the reign of God is near." Repent, turn, let go, surrender. "Lose your life and you will save it." Or from the Scriptures that fed his life: "Choose this day, whom you will serve."[29] "Choose life so that you and your descendants may live."[30] As with the first followers of Jesus, our search brings us to the point of having to make a decision about Jesus and about life.

---

29. Josh 24:15.
30. Deut 30:19.

2

The Decision to Follow

Peter, Andrew, James, and John, on the shores of Galilee, had to make a decision. Jesus had said to them, "Follow me, and I will make you fish for people."[1] The nature of the decision was clear: They could continue to fish for fish, or they could follow Jesus and end up fishing for people—whatever that meant. When we make a decision we do not know all that it may entail. This is especially true of a life-changing decision like the one put before these fishermen. They were being called from their fishing business and livelihood to follow Jesus into places and ways yet to be experienced. Matthew indicates the radical nature of the call when he tells us that Peter and Andrew "immediately . . . left their nets and followed him." And then, of James and John, "Immediately they left the boat and their father, and followed him." In Luke's version, "They left everything and followed him."[2]

On one level, Jesus was simply a rabbi gathering students. On another level, he was inviting followers who were willing to have their lives radically altered. The decision to follow this particular teacher was a whole-life, whole-self decision. This becomes clear with every situation where a decision to follow Jesus is contemplated. When a scribe approaches Jesus with the declaration that he will follow Jesus wherever he goes, Jesus indicates where he goes: "Foxes have holes, and birds of the air have nests; but the Son of Man has nowhere to lay his head."[3] Jesus speaks the truth here, not only about himself, the Human One ("Son of Man"), but all humanity. Jesus

---

1. Matt 4:19.
2. Luke 5:11.
3. Matt 8:20.

is saying that if we follow him into our true humanity, we will not be able to "set up house" for ourselves, as if our present existence were all there was and as if it were ours to construct in and of ourselves. Jesus leads us into a life that is always under the call of God and will take us in directions we could not have fathomed.

Another person who desired to follow Jesus said to him, "Lord, first let me go and bury my father." Jesus' reply made clear, in the face of this obligation, the central commitment for this disciple: "Follow me, and let the dead bury their own dead."[4] Relationships, as we tend to perceive them, become radically altered when we respond to this call. To a rich man, Jesus says, "Go, sell your possessions, and give the money to the poor, and you will have treasure in heaven; then come, follow me."[5] Just as Jesus called Peter, James, and John from their allegiances to business and family, Jesus calls this rich man from his idolatry of wealth. Give it away and then follow.

The radical response that Jesus called forth was in keeping with who he was, the one God had sent to bring liberation. As early Christians later confessed, Jesus was our liberator as he revealed and made present God's liberation. Followers came to regard Jesus as the expression of God in the flesh (the "Word made flesh"). However, when Peter, James, and John first decided to follow Jesus, they likely did not think in these terms.

What they were able to recognize was that Jesus was a man who taught and acted with authority: someone who had been divinely called and sent. They heard, in Jesus' proclamation of God's reign, a call to complete submission of their will to the will of God. Their decision to follow Jesus was, at the same time, a decision to trust God with their lives and identity. Deciding to follow Jesus was in some way also a decision about the nature of their relationship with God and about whom they would become.

Jesus, as they followed him, made clear how God's reign supersedes everything else, including the many "centers" we make of religions we construct for ourselves. We would place at the center, for example, God prospering us or God accepting us or God miraculously benefiting us. We are tempted to make religion into an exercise in how to get God to do a miracle in our lives. Of course, we do need miracles. We need what God does—which we cannot do on our own. But miracles are not at the center (otherwise they would instead be mere magic serving a false self). Jesus pronounces judgment on the inhabitants of Capernaum, Bethsaida, and Chorazim, because, despite all the "deeds of power" done in their towns,

---

4. Matt 8:21–22.
5. Matt 19:21.

they did not change their hearts and lives!⁶ They did not repent and enter into God's reign.

Søren Kierkegaard writes of two guides that we have: one calls us forward, the other backward. We are called forward to the Good (that is, to God), and we are called back from evil. This is the call to faith and repentance. And they cannot be separated. The call forward to trust God is also, at the same time, a call to turn to God, mindful of that from which we have come.⁷ Faith without repentance is not faith. We are turning from idolatry when we turn to God.

The steps these first disciples took came in response to Jesus' call, "Repent and believe, for the reign of God is near." We must keep before us this central message and fundamental decision. Those of us given the task of proclaiming this message must do so with a clear understanding of the false allegiances that take hold of our lives and the lives of the hearers of the message. We must take care not to supplant one false dependency with another.

In our own time, we hear preachers who have superimposed over the gospel a nationalistic ideology. So-called evangelical leaders have jumped on the Donald Trump "Make America Great Again" bandwagon, with all of its racist, oppressive undertones, because they share its allegiances. Their Jesus ends up sounding like an American nationalist and their message attracts those who would secure an American Christianity melded to an American (and often white) idolatry. From all such supplanting of God's reign with an idol, a false image that captures our hearts, we must turn away.

Jesus reserved his greatest judgment for religious leaders of his day, because of the ways they took aspects of the Torah and placed them at the center where God, and what God requires of us, ought to be. They replaced doing justice, loving mercy, and living faithfully with the tithing of herbs.⁸ They focused on outward things, while leaving their inner life and their central allegiance far from God. As a result they were full of self-indulgence.⁹

The word, therefore, is *repent*. Turn around. Come back to God. Turn from idols to serve a living and true God. Decide. Choose this day whom you will serve. Do not be like someone invited to a wedding feast who excuses

---

6. Matt 11:20–24.

7. Kierkegaard, *Purity of Heart*, chapter 2: "Remorse, Repentance, Confession."

8. "Woe to you, scribes and Pharisees, hypocrites! For you tithe mint, dill, and cummin, and have neglected the weightier matters of the law: justice and mercy and faith" (Matt 23:23).

9. "For you clean the outside of the cup and of the plate, but inside they are full of greed and self-indulgence" (Matt 23:25).

himself from attending because he just "bought a piece of land, and . . . must go out and see it."[10] Rather respond to the invitation. Come to the feast.

FOLLOWING THE WORD

For these first followers, there was a clear relationship between Jesus' identity and his message. Their decision to follow Jesus was both a response to the message of God's reign that he proclaimed and to Jesus as a person and a teacher. The radical demands of believing in the nearness of God's reign were mirrored by the demands of following Rabbi Jesus. Both God's reign and following Jesus called for a whole-self involvement. But both the reality of God's reign and the identity and meaning of Jesus' life awaited the daily following and receiving. More would be revealed only as they followed in obedience what they heard from their teacher.

This is what often happens for people today, especially as seen in those who come to Jesus from outside any particular faith tradition. They follow a trajectory somewhat similar to the first disciples, who were gaining clarity through Jesus' teaching. I recall a man in his forties, a journalist, a worldly man with little religious background, who decided to read the New Testament. I knew him before and after his reading. Somewhere in the Gospel of Luke and in the midst of Jesus' teaching, a light went on and his life was changed and redirected. There was something in his reading that reached out to him and took hold of him.

Something like that was happening to Peter, James, and John and the other disciples. They had a desire; they made a decision to be disciples of Rabbi Jesus, and, at some point, a light went on. We sense this when we read in the Gospels that Jesus asked his disciples who people thought he was. There were a variety of conjectures, and then Jesus asked them who they thought he was. Peter's answer—"You are the Messiah"—brought a response from Jesus: Jesus spoke of Peter receiving a revelation from his Father in heaven.[11] Like these first disciples, there are those today who, in their desire for God, are drawn to this same teacher through the witness handed down. They encounter a message that speaks deeply to their humanity, and they find themselves on a journey. On some level, they begin to follow Jesus' teaching. In the process of following, Jesus' identity and the meaning of his life takes on clarity for them. They become open to the fuller meaning that, for the first disciples, only came with Jesus' death and resurrection. There, they encounter the mystery of dying and rising: In Christ, we begin to die

---

10. Luke 14:18.
11. Mark 8:29; Luke 9:20; Matt 16:15–17.

to our attempt to make ourselves the center. We rise alive to the One who is the center and the source of our lives.

Our journey moves from following words to following the Word. A message takes hold of us and launches us into the reality of God's presence. The Word—God's self-expression—becomes flesh and dwells among us and within us. We share in that reality. We realize we are *becoming* a word; our lives, in the flesh, manifest the divine.

What we acknowledge here is that the first followers' journey is not so distant or different from ours today. Christ, in whom we encounter God, is made our contemporary through word and witness in such a way that we move from desire to decision. We find we must, like them, decide whether or not to follow Jesus.

THE DECISION THAT FAITH MAKES

Many years ago, on a college campus, I had a conversation with a young man. It was a conversation that led to a point of decision. In that moment, Christ was contemporary to this man. A desire and a significant degree of understanding were present. In regard to surrendering his life to God in trust and following Jesus, he said in essence, "I know there is nothing more important than this—to know God and to begin to be centered in the source of one's life—but there are other things I want to do first. I am afraid they would be taken from me." He was at the point of decision and he felt the radical nature of it, but in the end walked away from it. I met him again about a week later and found him to be in a very different place. His desire and understanding had shifted. Rationalizations and arguments had moved him from where he had been. It is difficult to simply stay with such a radical decision—stay with the struggle—without either, by the grace of God, saying "yes," or moving into a state of denial and dismissal, until God brings the issue again to the forefront.

This young man had begun to count the cost of following Jesus and it seemed too high. However, he was actually doing what Jesus told would-be followers to do:

> For which of you, intending to build a tower, does not first sit down and estimate the cost, to see whether he has enough to complete it? Otherwise, when he has laid a foundation and is not able to finish, all who see it will begin to ridicule him, saying, "This fellow began to build and was not able to finish."[12]

12. Luke 14:28–30.

That is how it is, in deciding to follow Jesus. There is a cost:

> Whoever comes to me and does not hate father and mother, wife and children, brothers and sisters, yes, and even life itself, cannot be my disciple. Whoever does not carry the cross and follow me cannot be my disciple.
> So therefore, none of you can become my disciple if you do not give up all your possessions.[13]

Jesus' appeal to count the cost of following him was a call for would-be followers to make a decision truly in accord with following him, a decision that took up the whole of their lives. Following Jesus demands our whole self. Better to sense the impact of such a decision, giving it befitting seriousness, than to take it lightly and end up with something that is a pretense for following.

We need today to hear this call to count the cost. We have found many ways to make following Jesus fit easily with our other predetermined commitments: allegiances to personal prosperity, cultural traditions, prejudices, attitudes to immigrants, national security, and so on. We are offended when it is suggested that the deep-seated and assumed legitimacy of such commitments have nothing to do with following Jesus and therefore will have to change. We have not counted the cost. The Jesus we have invented is not the Jesus that calls us to follow. It is a "Jesus" of our own imaginations, one that we want to have follow behind our idols rather than unmask them.

Better to count the cost. The young man mentioned above did some counting and sensed the depth of the commitment being demanded of him. There may come a day, in the midst of life's uncertainties and breakdowns, when he will again have opportunity to count the cost—and perhaps the cost will look different. He may even understand that there is nothing else worth living for.

We do not escape our desire to live from our source. We may attempt to live from various finite, creaturely realities, but they never fill our desire; we have to keep moving on to something else—until we are exhausted and realize the dead-end we have reached. At this point, we may again be faced with a decision, an act of faith sustained by the Spirit who calls us.

The kind of decision we face here is the foundational decision of our humanity. It concerns the source of our being and identity. It is the decision of faith, of where we place our ultimate trust. When we let go of our controlling self to God, we experience it as release and as a gift. It is an amazing grace.

---

13. Luke 14:26–27, 33.

I met with a couple who were struggling with drug addiction. I prayed with them and their young son in their apartment. Some months later I saw them again and they shared with me their "clean time." They said that the prayer in their apartment was the beginning of the change. God had done for them what they had been unable to do for themselves: God had released them. It was grace that had brought them to the place where they finally, in the words of the Twelve Steps of Alcoholics Anonymous, "made a decision to turn their wills and their lives over to the care of God." They were released into years of ministry to other addicts.

This is the decision that faith makes. It is a decision to turn our wills and lives over to God. When Peter, James, and John decided to follow Jesus, they were making such a decision, or were well on their way to making it. Their decision was, at the same time, the action of a gracious God. These young men were being lead into a way of life that was going to be shaped by their willingness to follow.

3

The Act of Following

Jesus lived from the Source: liberation and healing flowed from his life. Peter, James and John, Mary Magdalene, Joanna and Salome, witnessed this life from the Source and became participants. They followed a human being who was intimate with God, who called God "Abba" ("dear Father"), and revealed God in his serving others. By following him, they entered into the reality in which he lived. But coming to live in this reality required their "denying themselves, taking up their crosses and following him daily."[1]

SELF-DENIAL

Self-denial is simply an ingredient of the decision to follow. It is an aspect of this fundamental movement of faith. We have a sense of this in St. Paul's words, "I regard everything as loss because of the surpassing value of knowing Christ Jesus my Lord. For his sake I have suffered the loss of all things."[2] When we decide to follow Jesus, we decide to leave everything behind. Whatever we had looked to for life, wherever we had placed our trust, we now consider it a loss. In order to live out our decision to leave everything behind, we must follow Jesus daily, learning to deny to ourselves what we previously had depended on to give us life and identity. In the process, we are denying a false self, one that had its source in false dependencies.

Any disciplines of denial, any fasting, must be related to this fundamental self-denial. They must be reminders and helps to the self that denies

1. Matt 10:38; Mark 8:34; Luke 9:23.
2. Phil 3:8.

other allegiances in its determination to follow. The act of following, in and of itself, brings self-denial. Where Jesus is leading us, where God is calling us, requires us to deny whatever would keep us from following and responding to God's purpose for us.

Jesus got up in the early hours of the morning, leaving the comfort of his bed to seek a lonely place to pray. God's call upon his life demanded it. He then left the solitude and refreshment of prayer to go to a people who were like sheep without a shepherd. This next movement was a response to God's call to minister healing. Each movement in response to God's call was at the same time a movement of self-denial and leaving behind. So it is with us.

Self-denial is often experienced as a cross, a dying. It is a dying when we leave behind not only what was good in order to enter God's next good, but when we leave behind what took away from God's good. Again, Paul says: "I have been crucified with Christ; and it is no longer I who live, but it is Christ who lives in me."[3] The new life in Christ replaces the old life of making ourselves the center. The old life passes away and we are new creations in Christ.

We experience this daily as we die to misdirected imagined possibilities, so that we can live out God's call upon our lives. This happens for each of us, in ways particular to our individuality. Jesus had his unique calling; we have ours. We have gifts and creativity that God calls forth in service to others and to God's creation. We can hardly serve with the abilities that God has given us, if we are being sidetracked by disoriented attitudes, values, and priorities produced by false selves (false because they are constructed by a false centering). Therefore, we must die to those false ways and that false self. We must take up our dying daily. The act of following Jesus necessitates it. Following has us on a journey of dying, that we can also daily rise.

Our following Jesus takes us increasingly through a reorientation of our lives, as we face up to our false ways and the ideologies that justify them. Our ways and our thinking are in an ongoing process of change as we encounter Jesus' teaching and as we increasingly embody spiritual change. Both Jesus' instruction and the Spirit are our teachers, transforming how we perceive and understand and judge. The movement out of false ways is always a dying that we might *live*, a discarding that there might be new growth.

Jesus says, "Do not let your right hand know what your left hand is doing." We like to have others know what we are doing, when it means they may think highly of us. We also like to think highly of ourselves. This habit comes with constructing a self from a false center. Our thoughts quickly

---

3. Gal 2:19–20.

go to how we are doing, in our own eyes and in the eyes of others. Denying the right hand from knowing what the left hand is doing goes against the false construction of ourselves. Denying this false self happens only by God's grace; that is, by Christ's dying being formed in us. Our obedience to Jesus' words are always by the power of the Spirit. We are helped by a spirit of obedience—God's Spirit active with ours. When we turn from glorifying ourselves to glorifying God, it is due to the inner reality of God with us.

CROSS BEARING

Each of us must take up our cross and follow. There is no other way to grow as the children of God and there is no other way to live out our callings. We, as followers of Jesus, are sent out with the same mission as that of Jesus: Proclaim God's reign, heal, and liberate.[4] Go to people who are broken by sin and oppression, by disease and evil. Heal and liberate by the power of the Spirit. And let people know that God's reign is near. Call them to turn and to believe and trust in God's governing. Such a mission necessitates cross-bearing. As we engage in the lives of people who are harassed and beaten down, we find ourselves entering into their suffering. As we persist in ministering to them, waging a battle with spiritual forces, we will be carrying a cross.

Consider the description in the Gospel of Luke[5] of the seventy who are sent out by Jesus. They are to heal the sick and let them know that the reign of God has come near to them. (Where there is healing, God's reign is near.) This is their mission, but Jesus' instructions on how they are to carry out this mission lets us know what they are to expect of cross-bearing. They are being sent out "like lambs into the midst of wolves." They can expect fierce opposition. They are to travel light. They will have to trust their Father in heaven for daily bread. They are to stay focused on the mission. They are not to get side-tracked by stopping to converse with people on the road. When they are welcomed, they are to do the work of the kingdom. When rejected, they are to wipe off the dust from their feet and keep moving. They are not to fight against rejection, or take it personally, or change the message in order to be accepted, or to let their rejection become the issue. They are to move on to those who are ready to receive. Those who reject are to be left to God's judgment, not theirs. These followers are simply to carry on the work of Jesus, which is the work of God's reign: "Whoever listens to you listens to me, and whoever rejects you rejects me, and whoever rejects me rejects the one who sent me."

4. Matt 10:7; Mark 3:14–15; Luke 10:9.
5. Luke 10:1–20.

Those who follow Jesus can expect to suffer rejection (just as Jesus did). They can expect to carry the emotional and physical impact of opposition. They will experience their vulnerableness and need for God as their refuge and strength in the midst of disorder. Their cross will keep them going back to their source. God will provide. They have nothing else to lean upon.

Those who have allowed themselves to be sent out by Jesus know the experience described above. The message that calls people to turn to God, to trust themselves to God's reign, comes to people who have all kinds of other rulers in their lives. Aspects of themselves reign: their possessions, comfort, desires, control, status, power, self-image, and so on. Some, who are weary of the tyranny of these rulers, welcome being released. Others, who are held in bondage and yet in denial, fight release. For some, positions of power and privilege have so taken hold that they are willing to destroy others to maintain their control. They maintain power by oppressing and diminishing others. And their opposition is fierce.

The civil rights movement provided a clear view to the kind of brutality that is unleashed when power and privilege is questioned. Ever-increasing violence met non-violent protesters who confronted white supremacy and racism. Our idolatry—including the idolatry of whiteness—does not easily give up. It is for this reason, as Martin Luther King made clear, that change does not happen without struggle. New life does not happen without the cross, without going out as lambs among wolves, persistent, staying with the mission.

A Christianity that becomes comfortable with nationalism, militarism, racism, and xenophobia loses its soul in the same manner as a Christianity that is comfortable with hedonism, libertinism, self-indulgence, and materialism. Following Christ takes us away from a "my country first" in the same way as it takes us away from a "me first." When we, as followers of Jesus, call people back to their source, we are calling them away from the idolatry of self, ethnicity, nation, national security, possessions, power, and pleasure. When we name the idols that have us bound, we can expect pushback. At that point, we must simply take up our cross and keep following. Keep calling people to return to the source of their true selves, for the reign of God and their liberation is near.

OPEN TO TRUTH

> If you continue in my word, you are truly my disciples; and you will know the truth, and the truth will make you free.[6]

6 John 8:31–32

We are creatures that follow. We come after others into a world already in place. We come with much desire and receptivity. That desire and openness puts us on a trajectory for gaining knowledge—about ourselves, a world, and others. Without the world and others, we would not know ourselves. Our self-reflection is possible because of others and a world received through our senses. We follow after others who have come before us and, in openness to truth, we grow a self.

For disciples of Jesus, following is fundamental to life's journey, having to do with our ultimate goal. We follow the Human One into our true humanity. As in all following, following Jesus means being open. It is in openness and surrender to God's will that we are teachable and able to be led. Following has to do with receiving instruction and allowing ourselves to be guided by truth. And all truth is God's truth. We grow from received truth, from wherever it may come. In recent history, we, who are made out of star dust, have realized that we are situated in an evolving, changing universe. We have received a deepened awareness of our relatedness to all that is. Therefore, wherever we find truth, we know it is related to the Human One and to our humanity.

We often speak of "finding truth," as if truth were hidden or lost. Truth is everywhere: it is whatever is real. But we have the experience of finding truth because, from our birth, we have been on a journey of disclosure. Our experience has been that there is always more to be revealed. That is one aspect of finding truth. There is another: We can lose the truth. We can believe a lie. We can believe something that looks like truth, but has had enough reality stolen from it that it is no longer truth. This is true especially as regards our humanity, our true selves.

The issue is this: We can become closed to the truth. We can be waylaid and become disoriented, disillusioned, and deceived. In truth, this has been the experience of human history. The word "sin" points to this experience as a human condition. Being lost and blind are metaphors for this experience. In the words of "Amazing Grace," "I once was lost, but now am found, was blind but now I see."

For those who have come to see, following has to do with being, and staying, open to truth. Paul writes of a "veil over our minds" and then says, "When one turns to the Lord, the veil is removed." Then he writes the following:

> Now the Lord is the Spirit, and where the Spirit of the Lord is, there is freedom. And all of us, with unveiled faces, seeing the glory of the Lord as though reflected in a mirror, are being

transformed into the same image from one degree of glory to another; for this comes from the Lord, the Spirit.[7]

It is the Spirit that frees us from the veil. It is the Spirit that keeps us open, so that we are transformed into the image of the Human One, one degree after another. It is no wonder that the act of following is linked to anointing. Before Jesus moved out into his ministry, he was anointed by the Spirit. Before the disciples followed Jesus in taking up the mission given to them, they were anointed by the Spirit.[8] The "Spirit of truth," as John names the Spirit of God, provides spiritual sight. We are told in 1 John that God's "anointing teaches you about all things, and is true and is not a lie."[9]

It is by the Spirit of God that we are made open and receptive to the truth—the truth about *ourselves*. (Peripheral truths are easy to believe. "Two plus two equals four" requires little commitment to believe. Trusting ourselves to the source of our lives requires the commitment of our entire selves.) It is by the Spirit that we come to our true selves. It is by the Spirit that we are able to follow Jesus, the Human One.

Knowing the truth and following the truth of our humanity does not happen without being open to the truth—wherever it is found. If we refuse a truth because it would mean that we would have to change our thinking about the Bible, or about what we value, or about our behavior, or about our politics, then we in some manner close ourselves off from following. We close ourselves off from change and growth. The danger is that we have found security in something other than the truth; now, we defend what is false against the truth, when only the truth can secure us.

If we are going to follow Jesus into the truth of our humanity and into the actions to which he calls us, we must be open to the truth. Jesus and his teaching will upend us and turn the tables on us. Our philosophies of life will be questioned: the way we think of ourselves and others, our ideologies and our principles. We have spent much of our lives living a lie. We have lived as though we were the creator, rather than the creature. Following Jesus, truly taking in his teaching, is disconcerting, agitating, and life-changing. It tears down before it builds up.

If we have secured ourselves in a particular theology or ideology, rather than the God who holds our lives together, then we may run in fear from anything that questions our present ways of thinking. If we have structured for ourselves a way of living with which we are comfortable, we may seek to silence the truth of God's call and purpose that disrupts our ways. If truth

---

7. 2 Cor 3:17–18.
8. Acts 2.
9. 1 John 2:27.

is a cross to us because it is liable to unravel our philosophical and political commitments, we may decide to continue in what is false. Rather than be open to truth, we turn away to avoid its pain.

Spirit of truth, help us!

In discussing Jesus' teaching and Jesus as model, we must be clear that, in the case of following Jesus, there is no true following, no true receiving his teaching, no modeling his life, without the openness to truth that comes through self-denial and cross-bearing. Jesus' teaching, in one way or another, keeps calling us to die. His life, itself, confronts us with the impossibility of its being modeled without dying to what we have thought, acted out, and become. It is no surprise that, in the end, Jesus' first disciples followed the Crucified One. They came to participate in his dying that they might also rise with him, coming alive to God and to God's will.

DYING

Consider the ease by which we rationalize and justify our actions, the extent to which prejudices, biases, attitudes, and desires inform our thinking. Consider that we have heard lies from day one of our existence. Our growing up years were stimulated and informed by a wealth of viewpoints that came from false centers. And this is true for those growing up in homes of people of faith. It is true, because none of us can escape the false constructs of our human condition "in sin," as Christians have learned to express it. Maturing into our true selves only happens as we are re-centered, as we come to live from our source, because the truth is that we have spent much time with false centers. It is the broken condition of our humanity. We come into a disoriented world and are taken in by (and enamored by) its lies.

How we think about nation and clan, protection and security, need and provision, success and failure, goals and purpose, status and identity, power and prestige, are all given form and rationale from where our lives are centered. In the language of Jesus, what reigns in our lives determines how we live. God's reign is very different from the reign of personal power, possessions, and pleasure. God's reign clashes with all other such rulers. It causes us to see life differently than we had done previously.

We do not get very far in Jesus' teaching before our thinking and actions are challenged. Some teaching we simply do not "get," until we have followed Jesus for awhile. With other teachings, we are immediately tempted to argue with Jesus. If, however, we are uncomfortable with arguing, we attempt instead to reform what he says and to make it something we can live with. We are constrained to do this as long as we remain committed to our present "rulers," which give us our perspectives and ways of operating. For example, it is very difficult to come up with a "just war" theory from a simple and direct reading of Jesus' sayings. But it is not hard to understand why we have felt we have needed such a theory, living, as we do, in this world, with its allegiances and demands. As we encounter Jesus' instructions, we must be attentive to our tendencies to rationalize and justify our present positions. We must let Jesus' teaching expose our commitments and the source of those commitments, since "it is able to judge the thoughts and intentions of the heart."[10]

The point is this: We have much dying to do. It helps to know this. We should not be surprised that we are troubled with Jesus' teaching. As we are confronted with the truth of his life and teaching, we are having to face our lies. Those raised in churches may have to acknowledge how greatly their "Christianity" gives cover to all kinds of cultural traditions rooted in false assumptions. Coming to admit our false ways, we realize we must die. We must die to false thinking and doing. The death we die is the dying that Christ accomplishes. It is, as Paul tells us, a dying to sin and a coming alive to God.[11] It is necessary, if we are going to bear much fruit.[12]

The call to follow Jesus is a call to come and die, bear with suffering and loss, being open to the truth of his message and life and willing to do the truth. "Those who do what is true come to the light."[13] On the other hand, "all who do evil hate the light and do not come to the light, so that their deeds may not be exposed."[14] Consequently, Jesus says to those who could not accept his word, "Because I tell the truth, you do not believe me."[15] They would have to die, bearing the loss of their lives and their ideologies, as they had constructed them, in order to believe and receive the truth.

Jesus models for us the centrality of dying. He is our example of the essential nature of the dying we must undergo. We get glimpses of what death, his death, came to mean to him. He came to see that he was *sent* to die and that his death had meaning as "liberation (a ransom) for many," the fundamental act for one who came to serve.[16] At the least, he came to see what

---

10. Heb 4:12.
11. Rom 6:5–11.
12. John 12:24.
13. John 3:21.
14. John 3:20.
15. John 8:45.
16. Mark 10:45.

Paul saw: that "death is at work in us, but life in you." Paul was "being given up to death for Jesus' sake," so that life would be made available to others.[17]

Many scholars view Jesus' prediction of his resurrection to be an expression of the early Christian community, rather than that which Jesus saw for himself (beyond his expectations of a general resurrection). The early church, experiencing resurrection power and having the witness of the apostles to the resurrection appearances of Jesus, could easily read back into the gospel narrative Jesus' prediction of not only his death but his resurrection. Of course, given the extraordinary nature of prophetic and revelatory experience, Jesus very well may have seen something of God's purpose beyond his death. But a prophetic glimpse would nevertheless come amidst the darkness of death and his experience of abandonment. It is, therefore, worthwhile to consider what his embrace of death means, if little were seen beyond the cross—especially for the experience of faith.

When we stand at the grave of a loved one, we feel their absence. For people of faith, the "other side" may have come nearer, but the present distance from our loved one is complete. They are no longer with us. There is no more shared experience, except the shared memories with those who have known our loved one. If we think of physical reality as a manifestation of that which is spiritual, then death can be viewed as a final and complete self-emptying. Jesus' death can be viewed as the self-emptying that is ultimate trust in God: "Father, into your hands I commend my spirit."[18] Knowing little more than the death he is sent to die, Jesus trusts his Father in heaven. The death of Jesus, then, is seen as a giving up his life, an act of self-emptying: The Son of Man came "to *give* his life a ransom for many." "The bread that I will *give* for the life of the world is my flesh."[19] Jesus made clear that his life was not simply taken from him (it was that also), but that he gave his life in response to God's call.

What we see, in Jesus, is faith's submission to God's will, the trust in God that obeys God. He "emptied himself . . . and became obedient to the point of death."[20] Paul would have us see that we are to share in Jesus' life and, therefore, in his self-emptying. "Let the same mind be in you that was in Christ Jesus."[21]

Follower of Jesus, you and I have nothing to hold on to or protect. Our lives belong to God who calls us to empty ourselves. We do not have

---

17. 2 Cor 4:11–12.
18. Luke 23:46.
19. John 6:51.
20. Phil 2:7–8.
21. Phil 2:5.

to expend energy defending ourselves and "our religion." We do not need privileged protection from our government over that of the needs or protection of other religions. The governments of this world are in no position to be our protectors, not having the sense of who we are or what we are about, as we live under God's governance. God alone is our protector, guide, and sender, to whose call we now respond.

We are to live by faith, understood as surrender to God. Empty and open, we are free to love. Instead of protecting ourselves and "our way of life," we are ransomed, liberated to do God's will, to do justice, love mercy, and walk humbly with our God. We no longer have to try to lord it over others, get our way (or our religion's way). Dying to the old life, the ways of a false self, we are being set free to see the needs of others, to truly hear and respond to the cries of those who are oppressed. We are no longer simply bound to the perceptions our idolatries have given us—the idolatries of race, kin, gender, class, nation, power, wealth, and pleasure. As we die in Christ, we are set free to bear each other's burdens. We can hear and receive Paul's words, "Do nothing from selfish ambition or conceit, but in humility regard others as better than yourselves. Let each of you look not to your own interests, but to the interests of others."[22]

What would we fight to protect, when the interests of others are becoming our interests? This new direction that comes from following Jesus makes the needs of others accessible to us. We begin to cross over what used to be barriers between us and others, so that we can truly bear others' burdens, even the burdens of those whose experience is very different from ours. We are being given ears to hear what God is saying to us, including what God is saying to us through the cries of others, so that, in practice, we can love mercy, make right what is wrong and live in faithful obedience to God.

Dying, understood as self-emptying trust in God, becomes a way of life. Jesus says to us, "Come and die." Take up your cross and follow me. Lose your life for my sake and receive life. Die to living life on your own terms and come alive to God and to God's will.

In the following chapters, we let Jesus reeducate and redirect us—we who have been miseducated from a false centering of our lives. Jesus invites us to learn from him: "Learn from me; for I am gentle and humble in heart."[23] We have spent much time learning from the prideful of heart, including from our own pridefulness. Having decided to follow, we now lay down this false learning and desire to learn from him.

---

22. Phil 2:3–4.
23. Matt 11:29.

We have come to this point in the same manner as those first followers: We got tired of following after false voices. Our desire for God brought us to a decision to follow Jesus. We became willing to lose the false self of our own construction in order to receive our true selves from the source of our lives. Jesus is leading us to that source. We are ready to be taught. And Jesus' teaching touches on the various aspects of our lives, but now from the vantage point of life lived from our source. We recognize this in the first words of that collection of sayings we call the "Sermon on the Mount."[24] We realize, right away, in the "Beatitudes," that we are being taught something foreign to what we have received from the wisdom of the world.

---

24. Matt 5–7.

4

The Identity of the Follower

Blessed are the poor in spirit, for theirs is the kingdom of heaven.
Blessed are those who mourn, for they will be comforted.
Blessed are the meek, for they will inherit the earth.
Blessed are those who hunger and thirst for righteousness, for they will be filled.
Blessed are the merciful, for they will receive mercy.
Blessed are the pure in heart, for they will see God.
Blessed are the peacemakers, for they will be called children of God.
Blessed are those who are persecuted for righteousness' sake, for theirs is the kingdom of heaven.
Blessed are you when people revile you and persecute you and utter all kinds of evil against you falsely on my account. Rejoice and be glad, for your reward is great in heaven, for in the same way they persecuted the prophets who were before you.

Matt 5:3–12

Years ago, I was hiking above treeline in the White Mountains of New Hampshire along a ridge and over various peaks. The area was dry and I was running low on water. As evening approached I began to look for a place to camp at a lower elevation. I discovered a small stream and followed it to its source, a spring bubbling out of the side of the mountain. It was fresh, clear, and life-giving. I set up my tent there.

At the Festival of the Tents (Tabernacles), Jesus called all who were thirsty to come to him and drink.[1] He appealed to our spiritual thirst that draws us back to our source, to the living water. The above blessings or "beatitudes" put us in touch with the bubbling spring, the source of our lives and our blessing.

The first four blessings have to do with our fundamental desire as discussed in chapter 1. They are related to our essential neediness—our poverty, our grief, our lowly state, our hunger and thirst. In a world that equates our being "somebody" with having strength and power, wealth and possessions, and being satisfied and full, Jesus tells us that blessing is actually experienced at the point of our weakness and need. It is experienced at the point of our thirst for the spring of living water, at the point of our hunger for that life which comes from our source. Our need calls us back to our source. Everything else—between us and the source of our lives—will never fill us, will never give us our true selves. God comes to us through God's creation, but nothing of creation can, of and by itself, give us life and blessing.

The next three blessings, the subject of this chapter, have to do with our *being*. As we begin to live from our source, we become the merciful, the pure in heart, and the peacemakers. From the Spring of Life, we have received mercy and, from that mercy, we extend mercy to others. From our source, we receive singleness of purpose. Our hearts are becoming rooted in our true identity and calling. They are being purified. Being in union with God, we experience a uniting of the various elements of our lives, a wholeness, a peace with ourselves and others. We become makers of community and therefore become peacemakers.

The next two blessings are about conflict. In a world disconnected from its source, those who are reconnecting cause dissonance. Their lives call into question the values and priorities of a world that has lost its moorings. It is not surprising that they experience ridicule and persecution. They are persecuted for justice's sake.

In these verses, we are given the blessings of being—being that issues forth in works of love. These words give us the blessed identity that is ours when we live from our source. Our true identity is found at the point of the precariousness and brokenness of our existence, in our neediness for God. When we allow ourselves to be needy for God, we experience who we are as

---

1. John 7:37–38.

we receive ourselves from God. We are the merciful, the pure in heart, and the peacemakers. We are gracious, purposeful, and reconciling.

THE MERCIFUL

"*Poverty* of spirit" and "*hunger and thirst* for righteousness" express our desire for being, for the source of our being. "As a deer longs for flowing streams, so my soul longs for you, O God."[2] In that longing and openness, we receive our identity. Our true selves are a gift from God, expressions of God's grace and mercy. Therefore, as God is merciful to us, we become merciful. "Blessed are the merciful, for they will receive mercy." Being merciful and receiving mercy are one reality.

Jesus, who lives from God ("whatever the Father does, the Son does likewise"[3]), shows mercy. He is recognized for his mercy: "Have mercy on us, Son of David!"[4] Those who follow him must "learn what this means, 'I desire mercy, not sacrifice.'"[5] Following Jesus by living from our source, from the Merciful One, we receive *our* identity as merciful ones.

We long for, and receive, God's justice and we find that God's justice is marked by mercy. The follower, Paul, was clear on this. God's righteousness—the character of that righteousness—is recognized in "divine forbearance" and the passing over of "sins previously committed."[6] Any so-called righteousness or justice that shows no mercy does not come from God.

Receiving our being and identity from God, we experience mercy. Our very being is a gift. We exist by grace. And mercy is the gift we experience, no matter what we have done or how far removed we have been from our source. "Merciful" describes our identity, as we live from the Merciful One. God is like the waiting father who welcomes his prodigal son when he returns home.[7] As participants in the divine nature, we participate in God's mercy. We are no one's judge. We are in no position to hand down verdicts on anyone. It is this experience of mercy that enables us to do what Jesus tells us to do: "Do not judge, so that you may not be judged. For with the judgment you make you will be judged, and the measure you give will be the measure you get."[8]

2. Ps 42:1.
3. John 5:19.
4. Matt 9:27.
5. Matt 9:13.
6. Rom 3:25.
7. Luke 15:11–32.
8. Matt 7:1–2.

The followers of Jesus are recognized by their mercy. Their righteousness, as it comes from God, appears as mercy. A "Christianity" that stands in judgment of others, ridiculing and belittling others, is devoid of Jesus' leading. Its followers are led by their own self-made righteousness rather than by Jesus.

As we follow Jesus, we are being led into mercy. We experience God's mercy in the form of God's gracious rescue, healing, liberation, and forgiveness. We who experience God's freely given restoration of our lives learn to operate from that experience, so that with the same mercy we have experienced, we are merciful to others.

We also experience God's mercy, when we show mercy. Since we are commanded to love as God loves, we step out in obedience, depending on God's mercy to help us be merciful to others. As God empowers us to show mercy, we experience the mercy we are empowered to give. Consider the times we have experienced compassion for another human being and have felt that compassion to be a gift from God. We were graciously on the receiving end of mercy—a mercy that includes others.

Mercy sees the needs of others and it acts. It does not judge others because they are needy, or decide that they are undeserving of our care because of assumptions as to *why* they are needy. Mercy responds to need. And mercy sees what is needed, providing clarity for how to respond to needs. It cares. Hard-hearted "objectivity," "realistic" about what is wrong with people, is blind to what is actually needed. It is there simply to judge. Mercy, however, has eyes to see the plight of others, ears to hear their cries, and a heart to act. When we experience mercy, we know it is a gift of God.

Consider the story of Jesus and Simon the Pharisee. A Pharisee named Simon invites Jesus to his house for a meal.[9] While they are sitting at table, a woman, who is described as a sinner, comes uninvited into Simon's house, goes directly to Jesus. Weeping, she begins to "bathe his feet with her tears and to dry them with her hair," kisses his feet, and anoints them with ointment. It is an extraordinary scene! And yet Jesus receives her, allows her to minister to him in this way. Simon, on the other hand, is shaken and thinks Jesus could not be a prophet, as otherwise he would know what kind of sinful woman is touching him. Jesus, with prophetic discernment, speaks to what Simon is thinking by telling a story. It is a story about different kinds of debts and forgiving responses to debts. The greater the debt, the more the love for the one who is forgiving the debt. And Simon understands the story! Jesus then says to him, "Do you see this woman? I entered your house; you gave me no water for my feet, but she has bathed my feet with her tears

9. Luke 7:36–50.

and dried them with her hair. You gave me no kiss, but from the time I came in she has not stopped kissing my feet. You did not anoint my head with oil, but she has anointed my feet with ointment. Therefore, I tell you, her sins, which were many, have been forgiven; hence she has shown great love." Jesus would have Simon wake up and recognize what is going on in his life, in contrast to this woman he has judged. To the woman, Jesus says, "Your sins are forgiven."

We see mercy at work in Jesus' relationship to both the woman and the self-righteous religious leader. He responds to each, according to their individual needs. That is what mercy does. There is also another dimension to this action of Jesus. Jesus has followers who see and hear him. For them, Jesus is modeling the merciful life, both by his teaching and his actions. By sharing in his life, they are being changed into merciful people. It is the same for us, when we get past an easy "I accept Christ" and are truly baptized into Christ, united to his life.

THE PURE IN HEART

> "Purity of heart is to will one thing." (Kierkegaard)[10]
> "Purify your hearts, you double-minded." (James)[11]
> "For [God] is like a refiner's fire and like fullers' soap." (Malachi)[12]

Coming to live from the source, given our condition, is to enter a refiner's fire in which impurities, the elements of a false self, are being burned away, so that we are left with a true self, made in the image of our Creator. We experience ourselves as a bundle of ulterior and false motives (false to our true selves). It is our alienation from the source of our being that makes for this double-mindedness. In God, we discover our true selves and a singleness of purpose. We are in a process of being refined. The ulterior motives do not disappear, the false self hangs around, but we begin to recognize the false motives, as our purpose in life is increasingly being formed and defined from our source.

Purity of heart or singleness of purpose defines our true being, even as it is expressed in the midst of that which is false. Blessed are those who are gaining singleness of purpose, who know who they are and what they are called to do. Our blessing is in being who we are, as God calls us into being. When we pray, "Your will be done on earth as it is in heaven," we are praying

---

10. The title of Soren Kierkegaard's book: *Purity of Heart Is to Will One Thing.*
11. Jas 4:8.
12. Mal 3:2.

for our "coming to be." There is no *being* apart from the source of being. And there is no *coming to be* apart from God's purpose for our lives. "Not everyone who says to me, 'Lord, Lord,' will enter the kingdom of heaven, but only the one who does the will of my Father in heaven."[13] We must not think that Jesus speaks here of God's kingdom as only a reality after this life and distant from our present reality, ("up in heaven"). Otherwise, Jesus would not have said to the religious leaders, "Truly I tell you, the tax collectors and the prostitutes are going into the kingdom of God ahead of you."[14] The reign of God is *near*, to be entered *now* as our will comes to be directed to the will of the Father, and as we turn to God to receive the life and purpose God gives.

When Jesus tells stories of what the reign of God is like, he is telling us what we are like when God governs, when the purpose and intention of our lives comes from the center. Like the heavens that tell the glory of God,[15] our being manifests God. As with Jesus, so with us. Jesus, God's Anointed, lived this life under God's governance, so that we might live it also.

Jesus was very clear about who he was and what he was called to do. He came to know his identity and calling in the way we all do: desire, openness, decision, and being led by the Spirit of God. His coming to know God's will for him was a journey. It came through the process of growing as a human being, from infancy through teen-age years, to adulthood. The period of his life we know most about is that brief period of his ministry of proclamation and healing. Luke tells us that Jesus began his ministry at about age thirty.[16] This ministry lasted perhaps three years. It began with his baptism at the Jordan River, followed by a period of trial and temptation. Not long after he began proclaiming the nearness of God's reign, he chose disciples whom he trained to do the work he was doing. At some point, he realized that he was moving toward a death that would be "a ransom for many."[17]

We are given the impression that, up until the time that the adult Jesus began his work of proclaiming God's reign, he was doing the work of carpentry (although at some point he also may have been recognized as a rabbi).[18] During this period, he also was growing in understanding and a sense of calling beyond glorifying God in the calling of carpentry. Luke

13. Matt 7:21.
14. Matt 21:31.
15. Ps 19:1.
16. Luke 3:23.
17. Mark 10:45; Matt 20:28.
18. Mark 6:3. In Luke 4:16–17, mention is made of Jesus, in his hometown synagogue, being handed a scriptural scroll, which may have been a frequent occurrence as he was recognized as a teacher.

tells us that at twelve years of age Jesus was "in the temple, sitting among the teachers, listening to them and asking them questions."[19] He was growing into who he would become, in the same manner we all do: through listening, asking questions, being receptive, and gaining understanding. Jesus spent much time hearing, reading, and studying the Hebrew Scriptures, which is clearly reflected in his teaching. Jesus was being shaped and gaining clarity for that time when he would be sent out in active engagement, in a ministry of liberation to Israel and the world.

This pattern of growth represents a journey that can only be made on the basis of a singleness of purpose or purity of heart. It is this singleness of purpose—pressing "on toward the goal for the prize of the heavenly call of God"[20]—that enables Jesus to experience being sent by the Father. This is expressed numerous times in the Gospel of John.[21] Jesus is the Apostle ("Sent One") through whom all other apostles come to experience themselves as sent.

Jesus' followers shared in his life. Both Jesus' example and his teaching were changing them. This is what happens for present day followers as well. We are being changed as we share in Jesus' life and receive his example into ourselves. Communities of followers, as they follow, also become models in whom others encounter the single-purpose life, receive it, and are changed. For congregations to be agents of change in the world, they must take on the purity of heart of Jesus, the head of the gathered followers. Singleness of purpose must come to define them. It concerns their very being. Therefore, Paul encourages the congregation in Philippi to "live your life in a manner worthy of the gospel of Christ" by "standing firm in one spirit, striving side by side with one mind for the faith of the gospel."[22] By following Jesus, we become pure in heart, having a singleness of purpose.

And we are blessed, "for [we] will see God." This is the blessing of being open to God. We see God in creation, in others, and in ourselves. We see God in the work of God, in the gifts of creation, and in the serving and ministry to others that God raises up. And there is a future to our seeing. We reach out for it. "Beloved, we are God's children now; what we will be has not yet been revealed. What we do know is this: when he is revealed, we will

---

19. Luke 2:46.

20. Phil 3:13–14.

21. This expression of being "sent" is used fourteen times in the Gospel of John. One example: "The works that the Father has given me to complete, the very works that I am doing, testify on my behalf that the Father has sent me" (John 5:36).

22. Phil 1:27.

be like him, for we will see him as he is. And all who have this hope in him purify themselves, just as he is pure."[23]

THE PEACEMAKERS

> All this is from God, who reconciled us to himself through Christ, and has given us the ministry of reconciliation; that is, in Christ God was reconciling the world to himself, not counting their trespasses against them, and entrusting the message of reconciliation to us. So we are ambassadors for Christ, since God is making his appeal through us; we entreat you on behalf of Christ, be reconciled to God. [24]

Reconciled to God, we are taken up into God's work. God is *the* Peacemaker and all peacemaking comes from God. "Through [Christ] God was pleased to reconcile to himself all things, whether on earth or in heaven, by making peace through the blood of his cross."[25] The peacemaking into which we are called is the work of reconciliation involving both God and creation (including human creation). The two cannot be separated. As we are reconciled to God, we find ourselves becoming at peace with our neighbor and all of creation. Peacemaking always involves both God and creation. Otherwise, the result is an unstable and false peace.

Making peace is not merely "smoothing things over" because we are afraid of conflict. It is not a matter of "not making waves" so that we do not get ourselves in trouble. "Agreeing not to agree" may be helpful in many situations, but this does not achieve the peace Jesus came to bring. Jesus is our model of the peacemaker, yet the "prince of peace" could say, "Do not think that I have come to bring peace to the earth; I have not come to bring peace, but a sword."[26] Jesus the peacemaker overturned tables and agitated the very people who would eventually cause all manner of problems for him and his disciples. His actions made his followers concerned for his kind of peacemaking and they asked, "Do you know that the Pharisees took offense when they heard what you said?"[27] Whatever Jesus meant by peacemaking, it did not necessarily exclude conflict. It did not exclude the cross.

23. 1 John 3:2–3.
24. 2 Cor 5:18–20.
25. Col 1:20.
26. Matt 10:34.
27. Matt 15:12.

Peace, however, did mean *oneness* of the kind Jesus experienced, as expressed in the Gospel of John: "The Father and I are one."[28] That oneness between Father and Child is also to be experienced among the siblings. In his prayer on our behalf, Jesus prays that we be one, as he and the Father are one.[29] Paul writes of this peace when he calls the body of Christ to "be of the same mind, having the same love, being in full accord and of one mind."[30] But getting there does not happen without the struggle that involves a spiritual battle.

The truth is that all are one in God. The lie is that there is no god but ourselves. We reveal that we believe that lie: not by what we *say* we believe, but by how we live. We face a spiritual battle, as the truth faces off with the lie. The battle is with our idols, our self-made images—all extensions of ourselves. These images flow from a self playing at being its own creator. They take the form of our desires and attitudes, our "blood and kindred," our nation, our pleasures, power, and money. We attempt to make these aspects of ourselves the sources of our identity and the norms of our relationships.

This lie we live alienates us from our true selves, from our true source, and from our neighbor. God, our peacemaker, seeks to reconcile us to our true selves, to the human family, to all of creation, and to God. This reconciling work of God is what we see in Jesus. And we see the demanding nature of this peacemaking work. It demands that we fight the good fight of faith, which includes seeking out those who are lost, losing one's life in serving others, being willing to engage those who have power and are in places of authority, suffering and dying for the sake of others. God's peace is not experienced without struggle and change.

In the evening news, I saw a story of a white woman who moved into a largely black neighborhood and put up a pole with a Confederate flag. Her neighbors asked her to take it down, explaining to her what it meant to them. When she refused to do so, there were demonstrations in front of her house and others got involved—pro- and anti-Confederate flag people. Her neighbors, on both sides of her, built fences to block out the view of the flag. She put up a higher pole to keep her flag in view. And then she had a heart attack. Lying in a hospital bed, feeling the precariousness of her existence, she had a change of heart. Not knowing how long she had to live, she decided she ought to live it loving her neighbors. When she got out of the hospital, she took down the Confederate flag and handed it over to the head of an organization she had been fighting. When asked about honoring

28. John 10:30.
29. John 17:11.
30. Phil 2:2.

her ancestors who fought for the Confederate cause (her rationale for flying the flag), she said she was honoring them more than ever by loving her neighbors.

God was never mentioned in this brief news segment, but God was there. God is present when the reconciliation of neighbors happens, when neighbors are loved. It is often when we experience our finitude, along with our brokenness, that change takes place. We find ourselves before the Source of our being, the Alpha and Omega. We are no longer in control and become open to change. Peacemaking is God's work. When we begin to make peace, it is because we have allowed God to work in us. But it seems that we often first have to end up on our backs looking up.

This is true for individuals. It is also true for societies. It has become a truism: "change does not happen without struggle." True peace does not happen without a battle that, at its roots, is spiritual. Abolitionists understood this. Their fight for the abolition of slavery was a battle that had its roots in the oneness of humanity, a unity that comes from God who is one with God's creation. This unity could not happen without the disruption of the slave trade and the liberation of people enslaved, whether in the sense of forced servitude or that of servitude to the idolatries of racism and greed.

Jesus lets his followers know that they are blessed, as they live out their identity as peacemakers, with all that that entails: the losing of their lives, the suffering for the sake of others, the dying to idolatries and the rising to life received from the Author of life. Jesus' followers are peacemakers. That is their identity. Communities of Jesus' followers, when they are following, can be seen for who they are by what they endure for the sake of making peace.

Jesus tells us that peacemakers will be called "children of God," a term that has to do with the relationship of our being to the source of our being. Participants of the divine nature are makers of peace. They cannot be otherwise. Consequently, we must attend to our inner life—our relationship with God.

FOR JUSTICE'S SAKE

> Blessed are those who are persecuted for righteousness' sake, for theirs is the kingdom of heaven. Blessed are you when people revile you and persecute you and utter all kinds of evil against you falsely on my account. Rejoice and be glad, for your reward is great in heaven, for in the same way they persecuted the prophets who were before you.

The Greek word for righteousness ("dikaiosuné") in the above text shares similar meanings to that of the Hebrew words "mishpat" (justice) and "tsedaqah" (righteousness, justice) as expressed in the message of the prophet, Amos, "But let justice [mishpat] roll down like waters, and righteousness [tsedaqah] like an ever-flowing stream."[31] It carries both the meaning of being and doing what is right and the meaning of justice (making right what is wrong). Here, I translate dikaiosuné as "justice," in order to connect it more firmly with a dominant idea in the Hebrew Scriptures where Israel is called to give care to orphans, widows, and refugees. Consider these words from Exodus: "Then the Lord said, 'I have observed the misery of my people who are in Egypt; I have heard their cry on account of their taskmasters. Indeed, I know their sufferings, and I have come down to deliver them from the Egyptians, and to bring them up out of that land to a good and broad land, a land flowing with milk and honey.'"[32] Here God sees the misery of God's people, hears their cry, knows their sufferings, delivers them, and brings them to a good and broad land. God does justice and God's people are to do the same.

We are blessed when we are being persecuted for justice's sake. It is, of course, possible to be "persecuted" for unrighteousness' sake. I imagine the Pharisees felt persecuted by Jesus when he called them "whitewashed tombs with snakes inside." There was no blessing, only judgment, for them in this experience. Our blessing is in being ostracized for *doing justice*, for working to make right what is wrong. Furthermore, Jesus makes it clear that when we suffer for justice's sake, we are being reviled on his account. Jesus, like his Father in heaven, is committed to addressing wrong in order to bring about what is right. When we follow him, we find ourselves experiencing what he experienced. For healing a man on the Sabbath, "the Pharisees went out and conspired against him, how to destroy him."[33] As far as they were concerned, Jesus was breaking the law. In the book of Acts, his disciples find themselves in a similar situation, having been arrested after disobeying those in authority. Peter says to them, "We must obey God rather than any human authority."[34]

Follower of Jesus, do you see the injustice of our criminal justice system in the mass incarceration of people of color? Do you see the wrong of our nation's warring ways directed to maintaining its hegemony? Do you see the wrong that we do to the refugee and those seeking asylum? Do you

---

31. Amos 5:24.
32. Exod 3:7.
33. Matt 12:9–14.
34. Acts 5:27–32.

see the disregard for life, for the unborn and the born, for the weak and vulnerable and broken? Do you see the ways we diminish our humanity with our materialism and hedonism? Follow Jesus in calling out injustice and working to make right what is wrong.

As with all these aspects of our being, as expressed in the "Beatitudes," we must attend to our inner life. It is from our hearts that our actions flow. We must become mindful of ourselves and of what is going on inside us. With the help of the Spirit, we have to discern what is of God and what is not, acting in response to what God is doing in us and among us. "Go into your room and shut the door and pray to your Father who is in secret."[35] Attend to the source of your life that you may live from the Source. Don't talk about your faith. Don't make a big deal about "your religion." Attend to your relationship with God. Be present—alive to and acknowledging the Presence.

Those who drink from the Spring of Life affect the world around them. They are like salt that helped fire up the ovens in Palestine, in Jesus' time. They are like light in the darkness, not hiding themselves away. They let their "light shine before others, so that they may see [their] good works and give glory to [their] Father in heaven." The light that shines in the darkness is love—love that reconciles and heals.

---

35. Matt 6:6.

5

Following Love

What wondrous love is this, O my soul, O my soul![1]

Beloved, let us love one another, because love is from God; everyone who loves is born of God and knows God.

1 JOHN 4:7

As we continue to read beyond the "Beatitude" text of the "Sermon on the Mount," two things become clear: Jesus cares about our inner life (the intentions of the heart) and the centrality of love. Jesus does not come to take away God's commands, but comes that these commands may be fulfilled from the inside out. Anger and insult break the commandment against murder. Looking at another with lust (making a person merely an object of our desire) is committing adultery in our hearts. Out of the heart comes our actions: Calling a brother or sister a fool, or getting a certificate of divorce when we have lost interest in a partner.

Jesus would have us attend to our inner life. "For out of the heart come evil intentions, murder, adultery, fornication, theft, false witness, slander."[2] A change has to come to our hearts. The "word of the kingdom" has to be

---

1. American folk hymn.
2. Matt 15:19.

planted in our hearts, put down roots, and grow.³ God must reign at the center of our lives. "For where your treasure is, there your heart will be also."⁴

Therefore, "be on guard so that your hearts are not weighed down with dissipation and drunkenness and the worries of this life, and that day does not catch you unexpectedly, like a trap."⁵ We are to stay alert by means of prayer. We have inner work to do as we "welcome with meekness the implanted word that has the power to save [our] souls."⁶ The intentions and the centering of our hearts are a direct influence on the words that come out of our mouths and the actions we take.

The central reality for our inner life is that love reigns, so that actions of love flow from our hearts. Love must reign so that, in our relationships, we show mercy and compassion, do justice, and be peacemakers. Love is at the center of all of Jesus' teaching. It is the greatest and central commandment from which all others flow.⁷ Love displaces those intentions that would bring harm to another human being. Living from the source of our lives, from the God who is love, radically transforms our relationships. It is the only way for us to see ourselves in others and to embrace our humanity and that of others. Consequently, this love disturbs us. It unsettles and undermines the thoughts, feelings, and attitudes that stem from our ingrained, false constructs of ourselves, others, and the world. God's love is astounding in what it expects from us.

WHAT LOVE IS THIS?

> You have heard that it was said, "You shall love your neighbor and hate your enemy." But I say to you, Love your enemies and pray for those who persecute you, so that you may be children of your Father in heaven; for he makes his sun rise on the evil and on the good, and sends rain on the righteous and on the unrighteous. ⁸

With these words, Jesus places before us the radical nature of living from our source—from the God who is love. As with those gathered around Jesus, we also have heard that we should love our kin, our people, our nation, and hate

3. Jas 1:21.
4. Matt 6:21.
5. Luke 21:34–36.
6. Jas 1:21.
7. Mark 12:28–31.
8 Matt 5:43–45

our enemies. But Jesus says to all who follow him in living from their source that *no one* is to be excluded from their love. The God, in whom they live and move and have their being, provides rain for the unrighteous farmer as well as the righteous. Therefore, they are to love their enemies, even as God loves those who make themselves enemies to God. Jesus' followers are to do this "so that you may be children of your Father in heaven."

Living in obedience to these words radically changes all our relationships. If we are a people who "love our enemies and pray for those who persecute us," we will be regarded as a peculiar people and may even come to be identified with Jesus. Like Jesus, we will not operate by reaction, giving back in kind what we get, but we will "turn the other cheek." We will respond to others from the Spring of Living Water, the source from which we draw. These words of Jesus concerning our enemies are a piercing light that exposes the radical nature of following Jesus in this world. These words shine light on all the relationships in our lives. The love that is able to love our enemy is a love that is able to love our neighbor as ourselves. It is a love that can see the needs of the other, the Samaritan other, the one who is not our kin, our people, our nation, except insofar as love makes it so. It is a love that does not cause us to defend ourselves against the immigrant and refugee but rather causes us to see their needs and respond with welcome and help. Any rationale for not seeing their needs and responding with help comes from our false self—the one on which we have spent so much time constructing apart from God. When we operate from the One who always sees *our* needs and is ready to help, we find ourselves concretely welcoming others with the welcome of Christ.[9]

The directive to love our enemies comes early in these sayings of Jesus. I imagine that it came early in the instructions given to new followers of Jesus in the beginning days of the church of Christ. Right away they learn that following Jesus brings them into a radical new way of living. It turns the tables on the sentiments, motivations, and ways they have learned from the world and from its civil religion. It does the same for us. It can make new followers of those living in old "christianized" false constructs. We will find ourselves "exchanging the old wine skins for new." But Jesus' word calls for our obedience, our following. Only then will we walk into the new reality and experience and "see" it. Otherwise, we will remain stuck with our present rationalizations and ideologies. We will continue to follow our fears, biases, and present commitments.

On a personal level, loving our enemies means working for the good of anyone in our lives who have "crossed" us. Rather than react in kind to

---

9. Rom 15:7.

inflicted hurt, we are called to respond from the reality of what we are becoming as we live from the source of life and love. The God, in whom we live and move and have our being, gives us what we are to do: the loving action for the moment and for the person afflicting us. The action may be simply praying for the person—other options unavailable. Of course, those closest to us temporarily can become an enemy. Forgiveness, then, is the great gift that restores relationships.

This call to love our enemies speaks not only to our most personal relationships, however, but to our relationships within our community and society as they relate to other communities and societies. We follow Jesus and are part of a nation that makes decisions regarding enemies. And we cannot stop following Jesus in order to operate by the decisions of our nation. Often, in the face of decisions made from pride and power, decisions that call for reaction and violence, we are called to be witnesses to this "love of enemies." As such, we risk, at the least, being viewed as odd and, more likely, as subversive to the established order.

This love of our enemies that has us turning the other cheek will prevent us from taking up arms. Jesus would have us put our "sword back into its place; for all who take the sword will perish by the sword."[10] He uses "sword" also as a metaphor for doing battle. However, we have a different set of weapons: a *spiritual* armory as Paul concludes.[11] Jesus leads his followers on a path quite different from physical coercion as a solution ("kill or be killed"). His movement is revolutionary and effects the political order, as it moves forward—not by the power of military might, but by the power of God.[12] The early church demonstrated this in choosing to confront violent opposition with martyrdom, with a witness unto death. They further tended to the view that a follower could not be a soldier. In later centuries, following the Roman Emperor Constantine's "conversion" to Christianity, the church, as it became entangled with the state, moved far from this reality, toward notions of a "just war" theory—the idea that some wars and some ways of doing war are just. When "peace churches" arose, they were seen as "sects" outside the mainstream. But Jesus and his early followers *were* outside the mainstream.

We are quick to raise objections: What if an intruder enters my house? Am I not to defend my family by any means necessary? Are we not to protect our nation by any means necessary? (We have a president who has

10. Matt 26:52–53. Jesus, however, does speak of the sword as a metaphor for the division that takes place between his followers and those who oppose them. For a discussion of this usage, see Joseph, *The Nonviolent Messiah*, 26–29.

11. Matt 10:34; Luke 22:36; 1 Thess 5:8; Eph 6:10–17.

12. Joseph, *The Nonviolent Messiah*, 38–50.

raised the question of why we have nuclear weapons if we do not use them.) Our objections simply demonstrate that we are quick to justify our present "reasonable" positions. These positions may include notions of patriotism in time of war, national interests and security, and what we teach our children to do about bullies. Our present positions can end up being our excuses against actually following Jesus. What word will we obey? Jesus' word, or that of the nations of this world? It is no wonder that Jesus made clear that the dynamic of following him meant denying ourselves—our old selves (the ones that were constructed before we started taking Jesus seriously). The false self with its false positions must be abandoned, in order for the new self in Christ to come forth. The new self comes into being as we follow and obey. We must leave a lip-service "I accept Christ" as a means of ensuring that we go to heaven when we die, while, in reality, we have not yet come around to *following* Jesus. His teaching with regard to loving enemies makes clear that following him brings radical change to our thinking and our living—*if we do it.*

Will we follow Jesus, when following calls into question our most basic understanding and feelings about ourselves—who and what we belong to? Jesus' call to love our enemies causes a revolutionary reshuffling of our priorities and values. If we do it, we will be changed and we risk that all sorts of people—even some close to us—will oppose us. Like Jesus, we will become "signs that will be opposed."[13]

Throughout the history of humankind, going to war has been an integral part of nation building. It has been used to gain territory and power, to secure borders, to keep oil flowing, to gain control over resources, and maintain hegemony. It uses, as excuse and cover, threats to a nation's security and lifestyle, against which citizens must defend themselves and their nation. War, greed, power, racism, and fear are often combined with patriotism and national pride. Greed and fear of loss are powerful ingredients.

Jesus' call for us to love our enemies, turn the other cheek, and put down our swords is in keeping with his word about our possessions: "None of you can become my disciple if you do not give up all your possessions."[14] If we give up all our possessions, we lose much of what we defend. Our treasure is to be in heaven; that is, it is to be with the presence of God as the source of our lives, "where no thief comes near." There is no need to fight for or defend our true treasure. God remains the source of our lives and well-being, come what may.

---

13. Luke 2:34.
14. Luke 14:33.

We have learned from a broken world to divide up: "us and them," and "ours and theirs." But we learn from Scripture (from those who have come to know God as the source of their lives) that "The earth is the Lord's and all that is in it, the world, and those who live in it."[15] God does not make the distinctions we make. God shows no partiality. Jesus' followers continually receive that reality into themselves *as they follow*. That was Peter's experience in the house of Cornelius, where a non-Jewish people received God's word and the Spirit's anointing.[16] Peter came to realize that while he had previously learned "that it is unlawful for a Jew to associate with or to visit a Gentile," God now showed him that he "should not call anyone profane or unclean."[17] The fear of others taking what we view as belonging to us motivates all kinds of ungodly ways of relating to others. Fear of immigrants taking away "our jobs" will keep us from welcoming the sojourner, as God calls us to do. Fear of people with other religious persuasions taking away the position and prestige of "our religion" will cause us to speak in ugly and disparaging ways. Fear of the "other" (not our kin, people, nation) will have us acting in hateful ways. Jesus tells us whom it is appropriate to fear: "Do not fear those who kill the body but cannot kill the soul; rather fear him who can destroy both soul and body in hell (Gehenna)."[18] We are to fear God who is our judge. We are to fear and love God and live from God's presence, so that we do not fear what others can do to us and take from us and so that we do not act out of such fear of others. The dynamic of following Jesus and his teaching releases us from constantly feeling like we must defend ourselves. It moves us from fearful reaction to loving action.

The act of following Jesus takes us away from "us and them" thinking. When we start taking steps in response to what Jesus says to us, we find that we must deny ourselves, die to the old ways, and follow daily into a new way of relating—one that flows from the Spring of Love. Our attitudes must change. The intentions of our hearts must change. That only happens as we live from our source. Therefore, Jesus tells us that we do not obey the commandment "You shall not murder" merely by not killing someone. We break the commandment when we "are angry with a brother or sister" and insult them and call them worthless.[19] We break the commandment when we make them so "other than us" that they can no longer be loved by us.

15. Ps 24:1.

16. Acts 11:1.

17. Acts 10:28.

18. Matt 10:28. Gehenna was a valley south of Jerusalem where apparently there was a dump where trash was burned. It became a metaphor for God's judgment.

19. Matt 5:21–22.

Churches generally recognize and teach the love of enemies in personal relationships. If someone has made themselves an enemy to us, we learn from our pastors and teachers that we are to love and pray for them. We learn to forgive others. But then we may have to confront an enemy that has assaulted and brutalized us or murdered a loved one. At that point, we move to another level of struggle with forgiveness and love. It is a struggle with the depth of God's love, the kind of love we hear from Jesus when he prays from the cross, "Father, forgive them, for they know not what they do." It is the kind of love that we have, at times, witnessed from people who have experienced atrocities such as family members killed in genocides, but who, through much anguish and grief, came to a place of forgiveness. We are astounded by their witness. If we do not dismiss it as unrealistic or something we could never do or should not be done, then we end up in awe at the depth of God's love. We may even come to realize that this is how God loves us, we who have made ourselves enemies to God and who have allowed atrocities in our name as we have overlooked or even supported bombing campaigns and killings by our nation. (Consider, as one forgotten example, the general support of American churches and the World Council of Churches for the Korean War in which the carpet bombing of cities and towns by the United States in North Korea resulted in the death of 10–20 percent of the population, one to two million men, women, and children.)[20]

Jesus taught his disciples to put down their swords and love their enemies. And they followed. There is much opposition to the early Christian movement expressed in the pages of the New Testament, especially in the book of Acts and the letters of Paul. There are arrests and beatings and martyrdom. There are no accounts of disciples reacting with violence against those who persecuted them. This witness continues in the early centuries of the church. Ron Sider, theologian and social activist, has provided us with a collection of texts from this period that demonstrate the church's attitude to war (as well as to capital punishment, abortion, and infanticide). Here is a sampling:

> We who hated and destroyed one another, and on account of their different manners would not live with people of a different tribe, now, since the coming of Christ, live familiarly with them, and pray for our enemies. (Justin Martyr, c. AD 100–167)[21]
>
> We who were filled with war, and mutual slaughter, and every wickedness, have each through the whole earth changed our warlike weapons,—our swords into ploughshares, and our

---

20. Heung-Soo. "The Korean War and Christianity," 135–158.
21. Sider, *Early Church On Killing*, 24.

spears into implements of tillage,—and we cultivate piety, righteousness, philanthropy, faith, and hope, which we have from the Father Himself through Him who was crucified. (Justin Martyr)[22]

Those who formerly acted like animals and waged war on other people have now been transformed by faith in Christ. For he now tells in parable the gathering together in peaceful concord, through the name of Christ, of people of different nations and like character; for the assembly of the just. (Irenaeus, c. AD 130–202)[23]

The loud trumpet, when sounded, collects the soldiers, and proclaims war. And shall not Christ, breathing a strain of peace to the ends of the earth, gather together His own soldiers, the soldiers of peace? (Clement of Alexandria, c. AD 150–215)[24]

For when they know that we cannot endure even to see a person put to death, though justly; who of them can accuse us of murder or cannibalism? . . . But we, deeming that to see a person put to death is much the same as killing him, have abjured such [gladiator] spectacles. . . . And when we say that those women who use drugs to bring on abortion commit murder, and will have to give an account to God for the abortion, on what principle should we commit murder? (Athenagoras, d. c. AD 180)[25]

In this last quotation, we have references to several types of killing from which the early church excluded itself: capital punishment, contests that glorified war, and abortion. I am reminded of the words of former Cardinal Joseph Bernardin of Chicago, who spoke of the church's reverence for life as a "seamless garment" that included opposition to war, capital punishment, and abortion.

What if churches throughout the world, as followers of Jesus, were to follow Jesus in the way of the first followers? What if, with one voice, we were to witness against war as a solution to human discord and fear? What if we refused to go to war? Dietrich Bonhoeffer, pastor, theologian, and witness, envisioned something like this in his message to an ecumenical conference in 1934 in which he called upon the churches of the world to respond to Christ's command of peace to which they were bound "more inseparably than people are bound by all the ties of common history, of blood, of class, and of language." Brothers and sisters in Christ must obey

---

22. Sider, *Early Church On Killing*, 26.
23. Sider, *Early Church On Killing*, 29.
24. Sider, *Early Church On Killing*, 35.
25. Sider, *Early Church On Killing*, 31.

peace. "They cannot take up arms against Christ himself—yet this is what they do if they take up arms against one another!" Bonhoeffer notes that peace must not be confused with safety. "Peace must be dared." And who can know the outcome if it is—"if one nation should meet the aggressor, not with weapons in hand, but praying, defenseless, and for that very reason protected by 'a bulwark never failing'?" Bonhoeffer calls upon the ecumenical council to "send out to all believers this radical call to peace." We are left with the question of what might have been, if the call had gone out and believers had responded.[26]

Churches have often compromised with or have been co-opted by the political "realism" of a world that is alienated from its source. Has not the time come to leave aside the language of "just war?" Where is the "just war" being fought? With the exception of stopping genocide, where are the intentions just? And where is the implementation just? War has meant atrocities, acts of torture, large numbers of civilians maimed or dead, bombings of wedding parties, families killed in their beds in night bombings, children deeply traumatized, nations destroyed, soldiers coming home maimed in body and soul. How can we honestly say that the recent wars, in which we have been involved, have brought peace? They have brought terror and sown seeds for ongoing terrorism and social breakdown. Add to this the potential of a nuclear holocaust. In the midst of this reality, there are pastors, on the one hand, who support war with a Christianity subservient to nationalism and, on the other, pastors who remain silent because there are differing political views within their congregations. Is there no word from God in such times? No teaching from Jesus to his followers on peacemaking and peace witnessing?

The world needs not only individuals, but communities following Jesus. It needs the church to be the church. It needs pastors and leaders who will teach and proclaim a timely word and be willing to lose members. We must stop acting like *following* Jesus does not matter, or that it has only to do with personal relationships. Jesus called (and still calls) together a community of followers to be a witness as a community among communities—a witness to how sisters and brothers dwell in unity. We are to be a light in the darkness, a light to the nations. We are to live and speak the word of peace. We can only do that by following and obeying.

I am not attempting a rationale for pacifism understood merely as a position of principle or ideology.[27] I am simply calling attention to the

---

26. Bonhoeffer, *Testament To Freedom*, 228–229.

27. Bonhoeffer, *Ethics*, 221: "The point is not to apply a principle that eventually will be shattered by reality anyway, but to discern what is necessary or 'commanded' in a given situation. One must observe, weigh, and judge the matter, all in the dangerous

dynamic of following Jesus (and being led by the Spirit). It is not a set of principles we follow but the living Christ. We must take seriously every situation that calls for us to love our enemies and be peacemakers. We have to follow Jesus every time we hear a call to war from our nation, lest we make an idol of our nation. In following Jesus, we have to be actively loving our enemies, when decisions are being made for going to war. And church leaders must call members to follow Jesus rather than the voices of war—to work for peace, pray and protest, do justice and show mercy. If everyone who called Jesus Lord had followed Jesus rather than the voices for war, would our nation have been able to go to war so very many times in recent years? Perhaps money spent on instruments for killing would have gone to support humanitarian aid. And we would have prepared ourselves to assist in the work of peace and healing. We would have learned to work for peace, instead of prepare for war. What if we demonstrated, in unity, as the one body of Christ, how to make peace—demonstrated it before our nation and the world?

I realize there is a long "just war" tradition. Much of Christianity has embraced it. For many it is a settled tradition, if not a doctrine. In discussing where Jesus leads us in our relationships, I could have started with a less controversial teaching than "love your enemies," or I could have limited my application of this command to personal enemies alone. But the question I am raising has to do with where Jesus actually leads us when we stop rationalizing and start following. The early church seems to have been clear on where Jesus leads. Enda McDonagh and Stanley Hauerwas in their *An Appeal to Abolish War* call Christians back to their roots, reminding them of what Tertullian (c. 155–c. 240 AD) said, "The Lord in disarming Peter henceforth disarms every soldier."[28] This is where the church positioned itself at one time. What happened? We rationalized our way into the operations of power as it is conceived by a world alienated from God.

For the early church it was simple and clear: Followers of Jesus could not love their enemies and pray for those who persecute them, while at the same time kill them. Next to that straightforward love of enemies, the "just war" tradition with its complexity of argument and disconnection from reality comes off as what it is, a rationalization for nationalism, militarism, and war. It makes a case for a just war which humanity has demonstrated over and over again is an impossibility. On the other hand, many have viewed loving our enemy as an impossibility, even though there have been many people who have done it. All things are possible when we live from Love.

---

freedom of one's own self."

28. Hauerwas, *War and the American Difference*, chapter 4.

I was of draft age during the Vietnam War. I knew I could not go to Vietnam and shoot and kill Vietnamese. The false premises for the war and the reality of it not being a "just war" mitigated against it. I had also become serious about following Jesus and knew Jesus was not leading me to kill other human beings halfway across the world. My nation was leading me to do that, but not Jesus, God's Anointed. When my draft number came up, I was further pressed to decide about war generally as a solution to seemingly intractable security problems, as conceived and defined by nations. I was pressed to ask if Jesus ever leads us into war. My government only recognized conscientious objection to war in general. My opposition to the Vietnam War was not enough of a conscientious reason for my draft board. I talked to two pastors that I respected. Neither were pacifists. One counseled against conscientious objection. The other encouraged me to listen to my conscience. I would have to do what I felt the Spirit was leading me to do, regardless of what others thought and taught. His answer freed me. It freed me to listen to Jesus' commands and the leading of the Spirit, rather than the heavy weight of the "just war" tradition of my denomination. What I discovered is that the witness of Jesus in the New Testament provided a foundation for peacemaking rather than a justification for war. Followers of Jesus were called into a radically new way of living, under God's governance, to which they were to give witness. Conscience and the teaching of Jesus was the way forward. I felt constrained to simply follow where Jesus and the Spirit led. That meant giving attention to my inner life, the centrality of love, and what Jesus called me to do when he said "love your enemies" and "be peacemakers." I was also grateful for a history of peace churches and peacemakers whose actions paved the way for legislation that would recognize conscience (although, to this day, selective conscientious objection is not recognized). Their witness allowed me to choose to do alternate civilian service, working with youth.

Much of what passes for Christianity has been acculturized to nationalism and militarism. We need to be re-christianized! We need to encounter Jesus, not as a distant ideal, but as the Human One who leads us into our true humanity. It is Jesus, God's Anointed, that we must listen to now. This means there must be a new "now" for us. The first followers of Jesus realized very quickly that they were on a journey into a new way of being. The old was passing away and all was new. Those that gather in our churches must become contemporaries of the living Jesus, following him daily, dying to the old ways and rising to the new. Christian leaders must expect for themselves, and for those they serve, a conversion that touches every aspect of their lives, so that dying daily becomes less a surprise and more a way of life.

Certainly, pastors and communities of faith that are committed to following Jesus in loving enemies must reach out and minister to people where they are, in the context of their lives in a nationalistic and militaristic environment. Jesus responded to the centurion's plea for him to heal his servant. He did not speak to him moralistically, telling him he ought not be a soldier. Christ and his followers meet and respond to people at the point of their need, knowing that more will be revealed as their journey continues. However, leaders especially, as they lead communities into the reality of peacemaking, must make plain what loving enemies involves. Those who come into such communities, through the experience of God's healing, then encounter the radicalness of God's love in peacemaking and refusal to participate in war. They are given the opportunity to choose to be witnesses to this love of God, as they are changed by the act of following Jesus. Among those aspects of their lives that they are being led away from is their warring ways.

We can start at any point in Jesus' teaching and we will be changed as we follow—as we simply step out, even with doubts and fears, and follow. Following Jesus by concretely loving enemies and becoming peacemakers will have us taking up the cross we are given to carry. It will have us turning away from the false self of our own construction for the new life in Christ. If, on the other hand, we persist in our warring ways and rationales, then the honest thing would be to acknowledge our opposition to Jesus' teaching on loving enemies and our refusal to follow where he leads. Better this than to give lip-service to Jesus as Lord while actually committed to follow our feelings of bitterness toward personal enemies and, on a social level, follow nationalistic impulses directed to "national security" and "our people" and our nation's power over other nations.

Acting from the kind of love that loves enemies provides a foundation for all forms of loving. This love moves beyond tribe and kin to see people in need throughout our diverse humanity. It feeds the hungry, gives a cup of water to the thirsty, clothes the naked, and visits the sick and the imprisoned. In these acts of loving the "least," as Jesus calls them, the least in power to give in return, we are ministering to Jesus.[29]

When we grow in loving our enemies, all our relationships change. Intimate relationships change as we grow in caring for the welfare of others in our lives and for their living out their own callings. Love has us supporting, encouraging, forgiving, and suffering with others. Love does not turn others into merely objects of our desire. Lust does that; love does not. In a world where our desires become lust and lust sidetracks us and directs our

---

29. Matt 25:31–46.

actions, Jesus calls us back to the source of life and action. As we become rooted in love, we find ourselves living counter to a pervasive culture of unhealthy habits.

Furthermore, the followers of Jesus must not build a wedge between the personal and social. On the face of it, some values of Jesus' community may appear "conservative," others "progressive." But, in their depths, they will have another source than that of mere ideology. The love that makes possible enduring personal relationships is the same love that remains steadfast in doing justice and showing mercy. At both the personal and social levels, the followers of Jesus, like Jesus, will be "signs that contradict" the prevailing ways of the world.

And love does not judge others. It discerns, but it does not pass judgment. It does not condemn. It discerns what is loving from what is not. It is wary of "false prophets, who come . . . in sheep's clothing but inwardly are ravenous wolves."[30] Love knows them by their fruits and will warn others. But love does not use up energy condemning others. Instead it judges the true from the false, in order to do what is true and call out what is false. Love operates by truth.

That love does not judge others means that love sees prejudices and moves past them. We are socialized into prejudices, but love chooses not to operate by prejudices and thus releases us from prejudice. Some have suggested that Jesus is having to deal with a prejudice, a socialized view of those outside the Jewish community, when approached by a Syrophoenician woman.[31] As with us, his growth happened within a particular society which placed limits on how to view his mission and the expansiveness of God's reign. The Syrophoenician woman challenged Jesus to expand his sense of calling. She begged him to deliver her daughter from an evil spirit, but Jesus said to her, "Let the children be fed first, for it is not fair to take the children's food and throw it to the dogs." Now, we may be tempted, by our discomfort, to clean up Jesus' reference to her as a dog by saying that he was simply testing her. It seems more likely, however, that Jesus' socialized perspective on his mission was being tested. Having viewed his call as limited to the children of Israel, he is now receiving a way forward into God's expansive call through his encounter with this woman. The Gentile woman says to Jesus, "Sir, even the dogs under the table eat the children's crumbs." Jesus listens and receives the implication of her words. He responds with, "For saying that, you may go—the demon has left your daughter." What was it in this woman's words to which Jesus responded? William Placher, in his

---

30. Matt 7:15–16.
31. Mark 7:24–30.

commentary on Mark, gives us Luther's words: "She catches Christ with his own words. He compares her to a dog, she concedes it, and asks nothing more than that he let her be a dog.... Where will Christ now take refuge. He is caught."[32] In her need, in her love for her daughter, this woman remains open to Jesus, ready to receive, no matter what he may call her. She will accept being called a dog if it means that a crumb of healing will fall to her daughter. Jesus sees her faith and acts in response to her need, rather than from a socialized attitude or perspective. Love sees the need and responds, and Jesus grows in his vision of God's reign. Jesus shares in the limits and the brokenness of our societies, so that we may share in his openness and growth. In him, there is liberation from prejudicial attitudes and actions. Following Jesus takes us into a love that listens to the needs of others, rather than to our prejudices, and then acts for the sake of the other. It is racism—the idolatry of race—that keeps us bound. Racism is the stance that makes our ways and thinking the norm and standard by which we judge others. Racism provides a rationale for our prejudicial attitudes. God's reign of love releases us from the idolatry of race. The love of God poured into Jesus' heart by the Spirit enabled him to hear the pleas of the Syrophoenician woman despite the limits of Judean society. In Christ, that same love, poured into our hearts, enables us to truly listen to others, rather than to our own in-turned thoughts and feelings about others or the socialized limits placed on us. Acting on the love of God, for the sake of others, changes our thoughts and feelings. For example, those of us who are white can be made able to hear black young people, who march and call for an end to police violence, in the same manner that we are able to hear white students call for a change in gun laws in response to mass shootings in schools. When love acts, we change, our perceptions change.

    I was preaching at a church in a small town in rural Minnesota. A member of the church asked about the riots in Chicago where I pastored a congregation. This was following the shooting of Michael Brown by a police officer in Ferguson, Missouri. I was surprised by the question and my surprise must have registered on my face, because this member's face registered anxiety that he may have said something wrong. I simply let him know that there were no riots, but there were strong, loud, peaceful protests and some civil disobedience. There were members of my congregation who took part in these actions. This man had a desire to understand. But he lived at a great distance from these happenings and news sources clouded or slanted the story told. More to the point, our racism, and the racism of our society,

---

32. Placher, *Mark*, 6:14–8:26.

affects our perceptions. Black protesters look different from white protesters when our perception is skewed by racism.

How do such perceptions change? The change happens as we turn over our lives to the reign of God, so that the love of God can begin to reign in our hearts and displace the idolatry of race. It happens as the love of God enables us to move past disoriented perceptions and truly listen to others, letting us hear and respond to the reality that others experience. Frank Thomas reminds us of how important it is "to look to the moral imagination of the marginalized, disenfranchised, and vulnerable in any society and culture."[33] Their moral imagination will help us. Love will take up what we receive, so that we will act for the sake of others and, in acting, bring change to ourselves and our society.

LOVE ACTS

> One of the scribes came near and heard them disputing with one another, and seeing that he answered them well, he asked him, "Which commandment is the first of all?" Jesus answered, "The first is, 'Hear, O Israel: the Lord our God, the Lord is one; you shall love the Lord your God with all your heart, and with all your soul, and with all your mind, and with all your strength.' The second is this, 'You shall love your neighbor as yourself.'"[34]

Love is commanded. We are commanded to love God with our whole selves and to love our neighbor as ourselves. Feelings of compassion and mercy help love, but simply feeling compassion is not enough. Action is needed. Jesus tells a story of a priest and a Levite, who, on seeing a man beaten and dying, pass on the other side of the road, while a Samaritan, an outsider, stops and bandages his wounds and provides for his needs. The priest and the Levite may have felt something, but the Samaritan did something. Love is commanded because it involves action; it acts in response to the needs of the other.

Love also is commanded because love has to do with our true selves. The command to love God and neighbor is a calling forth of our being, as God created and liberated us to be. In the above quote, after Jesus answers the scribe's question by saying the greatest command is the command to love God and neighbor, the scribe says to him, "You are right, Teacher; you have truly said that 'he is one, and besides him there is no other'; and 'to

---

33. Thomas, *How To Preach*, 388, Kindle.
34. Mark 12:28–31.

love him with all the heart, and with all the understanding, and with all the strength,' and 'to love one's neighbor as oneself,'—this is much more important than all whole burnt offerings and sacrifices." Then we read: "When Jesus saw that he answered wisely, he said to him, 'You are not far from the kingdom of God.'"[35] By this man's understanding, Jesus sees that he is not far from the source, from God's giving and governing of his life. This love of God that loves the neighbor flows from the source of our being in God. It comes of being a child of God. God's command is a call to be who God created us to be, by God's empowering.

Love acts in response to the needs of the other, including the other's need for God and for growth as a child of God. In Jesus, we see that where healing is needed Jesus responds with healing. Where deliverance is needed, Jesus liberates. Where challenge is needed, Jesus challenges. We even see in Jesus' words of judgment an act of love. When he calls out religious leaders with harsh words ("You are like whitewashed tombs, which on the outside look beautiful, but inside they are full of the bones of the dead and of all kinds of filth."[36]), he calls them from their hypocrisy and the denial of their condition. He challenges them both for their own sake and for the sake of those on whom they lay heavy burdens. Jesus' warnings are acts of love. We live in a time when Christian leaders must challenge other Christian leaders who lead people astray with a nationalist and racist idolatry, or a false prosperity gospel, or legalistic judgmentalism. Those who name the name of Christ, but have moved far from the good news of Jesus, must be held to account for their false messages. A warning must go out so that others are not fooled by false teachers and false prophets. We see, in Jesus, that love warns others. ("Beware of false prophets, who come to you in sheep's clothing but inwardly are ravenous wolves. You will know them by their fruits."[37])

Jesus, who overturns the tables of money changers in the temple, makes clear that love is not a matter of being nice. It acts in response to the need it encounters. The tables of the money changers needed to be turned over in a prophetic and symbolic action that focused attention on the idol that had been placed at the center of a people's worship. Certainly, Jesus leads followers today to call out the idolatry that displaces the worship of the one God. When a nationalistic and false gospel raises up a nation and its values above other nations and peoples, allowing the atrocities of war in its name, it has to be called for what it is: a false Christianity. Or, when "sowing seeds" to get God's blessing, a blessing that looks much like the

---

35. Mark 12:32–34.
36. Matt 23:27.
37. Matt 7:15–16.

values marketed in American media, then it has to be named for what it is, a false Christianity. Following Jesus is not sowing seeds to get a blessing; it is doing God's will to God's glory. When God's will is done by the love of God poured into our hearts as a gift, then there is light in the darkness. People get to see what the love of God looks like. They see people being healed and delivered. They see that what is wrong is being made right and that those who are broken have mercy shown toward them rather than condemnation.

Love acts for the sake of others. The love of God, made manifest in Jesus, moves us out to the outcasts, to the poor and passed over, to the refugee, the homeless, the hurting, and the neglected. And this is where Jesus leads us. How is God's love seen in hateful rhetoric against Muslims or those of other religions? How is God's love known by "throwing stones" at other sinners (whose sin we have decided is worse than ours, when all have sinned)? How is God's love seen in demeaning the poor by referring to some as the "deserving poor" as if everything were not a gift (and as if we had not taken hold of the gifts that were meant for others)? Love welcomes and encourages and provides hope. It raises up others who have fallen. It bears burdens, rather than adding to them. It does justice. It works to right what is wrong in the way nations operate. And it engages others to do likewise.

Jesus gathers together followers who will learn to love one another and, in so doing, reveal to the world God's love: "By this everyone will know that you are my disciples, if you have love for one another."[38] The world needs to see communities of love that welcome others into that same love. Jesus' communities are meant also to be training centers for moving out to the world in love. Jesus gathers followers in order to send them out. They are to love by serving, bearing burdens, entering into the suffering of others, showing mercy, doing justice, "overturning tables," confronting, challenging, witnessing, working to make right what is wrong.

---

38. John 13:35.

6

The Gathering of Followers

Jesus gathered followers. Sometimes he had "the twelve" with him, twelve men along with women: Mary Magdalene, Joanna, Susanna, and many other women.[1] Sometimes he was with his inner circle of Peter, James, and John. Sometimes the gathering was much larger, seventy or more. Paul tells us that the risen Jesus appeared to over five hundred followers at one time. Jesus created church. The Greek word (ecclesia) that gets translated "church" simply means *gathering*. If we read "gathering" every time we read the word "church" in the New Testament, we would get a feel for what Jesus was doing and what the Spirit of Christ continues to do.

Jesus gathered followers in order to send them out.[2] He did not create an organization for preserving a set of doctrines or principles to live by, or a repository for cultural traditions. The assembly (ecclesia) of followers that he called together was formed for the liberating experience and work of God's reign. Jesus engaged them in the work he was doing. He sent them out with authority to heal and proclaim the nearness of God's reign and call people back to God.[3]

The gospel witness makes it clear that the followers of Jesus were gathered for the sake of action in the world. Jesus was about action, and those who followed him were engaged in action. A congregation that carefully instructs people in its doctrines, gives care to the order and beauty of its worship service and prides itself in its internal "fellowship," but is not

1. Luke 8:1–3.
2. "Follow me and I will make you fish for people" (Mark 1:17).
3. Mark 6:6–12; Luke 9:1–6, 10:1–17.

engaged in the world in healing, liberation, and witness to God's governance is not yet a gathering of Jesus Christ, for Jesus gathers in order to send out.

The depiction of Jesus' gathered followers that we receive in the Gospels is a sign that contradicts much of what goes for church in the United States of America. Jesus does not gather his followers together to create a worship center where they receive a dose of motivational speaking and learn how to sow seeds for health, wealth, and success. Jesus does not gather people for the purpose of maintaining traditions and doctrines, or to be a moral anchor of society, or to operate as an organizing meeting. Jesus gathers followers for the centering of their lives, so that they are empowered to go out as witnesses to God's reign.

Jesus' followers are gathered for worship "in Spirit and in truth," which empowers their going out. Yes, within the gathering there is instruction, but it is instruction that moves followers outward in their relationship to God and to others. Yes, the gathering has a moral dimension, but its ways of being in the world are an offense to the pridefulness of the world. The gathering organizes for action, but it is activated by the Spirit rather than an ideology. Yes, God prospers God's people, but God's blessing is in God's will, not in "seeds sown" to manipulate God. Jesus' assembly is to be the embodiment of God's love. And God prospers it in loving service to others.

God so loved the world that he sent his Son, and Jesus prays, "As you have sent me into the world, so I have sent them into the world."[4] Calling churches, which have lost their way, back to this reality means calling them back to God. "Turn back to God and have faith, for God's reign is near." God alone will turn our hearts to God, and God alone will open our eyes, empower, activate, and send us out to minister to a broken world. Without God, as the source of our lives, there is no going out with the power of God to do the work of God. As we consider these first followers gathered around Jesus, we do so with the awareness that this gathering is the action that prepares them for action out in the world.

At the forefront of activity in the Gospels is the action of proclaiming, teaching, healing, and liberating. In the background is Jesus and his followers going away "to a deserted place by themselves" to pray.[5] Prayer, instruction, and training in "fishing for people" were at the core of their gatherings.

---

4. John 17:18.

5. Mark 6:32. The text does not include "to pray," but I assume it. Reference elsewhere is made to Jesus going to deserted places to pray. See Luke 5:16.

FROM PRAYER TO ACTION

Jesus modeled a life of prayer. From the Gospel of Luke we learn that Jesus "would withdraw to deserted places and pray."[6] Before he chose his core group of twelve, "he went out to the mountain to pray; and he spent the night in prayer to God;"[7] Before asking them, "Who do the crowds say that I am?," he "was praying alone, with only the disciples near him."[8] And he took Peter, James, and John up a mountain to pray.[9]

Jesus taught about prayer. Again, from the Gospel of Luke: "He was praying in a certain place, and after he had finished, one of his disciples said to him, 'Lord, teach us to pray, as John taught his disciples.'" What follows is Luke's version of the "Lord's Prayer." Jeffrey Gibson has pointed out that it is more accurate to call it the "Disciples' Prayer," since this is what Jesus taught his followers to pray.[10] Both the Luke and Matthew versions have at their core a prayer for God to reign (and therefore God's will to be done) and that God would keep us steadfast in the time of trial, so that we would remain faithful in doing God's will.

Jesus taught his followers to persist in prayer. Keep on asking, seeking, and knocking, "for everyone who asks receives, and everyone who searches finds, and for everyone who knocks, the door will be opened."[11] With prayer comes the Holy Spirit: "If you then, who are evil, know how to give good gifts to your children, how much more will the heavenly Father give the Holy Spirit to those who ask him!"[12] Jesus' followers are to "pray always and not to lose heart."[13] They are to pray from a position of need: "God, be merciful to me, a sinner!"[14] They are to be "alert at all times" in prayer.[15] Before his arrest and trial, Jesus spent time praying, telling his followers, "Pray that you won't give in to temptation."[16] Luke informs us that it was Jesus' "custom" to go to the Mount of Olives to pray. We are given the impression that it was not only because of what he was facing in that particular moment. It was a way of life within which he included his followers.

6. Luke 5:16.
7. Luke 6:12.
8. Luke 9:18.
9. Luke 9:28.
10. Gibson, *The Disciples' Prayer*, 1–13.
11. Luke 11:5–13.
12. Luke 11:13.
13. Luke 18:1.
14. Luke 18:9–14.
15. Luke 21:36.
16. Luke 22:40 CEB.

Mark and Matthew make reference to Jesus and his followers singing songs of praise as they end their Passover meal, before they make their way to the Mount of Olives and Gethsemane. We get a glimpse of a community of Jesus and his followers celebrating festivals of faith, reenacting God's acts of liberation, praising God, and spending time in prayer. It is critical that we firmly grasp the source of action for Jesus and his followers. Their public ministry, the works of healing and acts of liberation, and the confrontation with those in positions of authority do not arise from a particular ideology or philosophy. They are the result of learning to live in the presence of God. It is from the source of their lives, from incomprehensible mystery, that they receive power and discernment which is the basis of their action.

For followers, today, prayer remains the root of our action. Prayer "in the Spirit" or worship "in spirit and in truth" forms the basis of gathering and sending, for it makes following possible.[17] If we follow Jesus, we are gathered into community and then sent out, the Spirit helping us to faithfully obey. Therefore, the community that Jesus gathers is a community of the Spirit—of word and Spirit. In obedience to the incarnate Word, to the teaching, to the discerned timely word, to the Spirit's leading and empowering, the sent community takes form.

But this movement into becoming a sent community means that the church, as it exists today, will undergo change. We can expect congregations will go through a kind of "deculturalization" when it comes to a *church culture* informed by the prevailing culture of the world. Much of what is practiced by many congregations is an amalgamation of religious values with national values and priorities, racialized thinking, and societal attitudes toward possessions, security, and power. Churches often exhibit a culture that has lost its roots in the Christ reality. The light of the Anointed One fails to shine. Jesus' first followers became lights in the world by following the Light of the world. The deculturalization that must take place for the light to again break into the darkness can happen only by following Jesus, being obedient to his direction as witnessed in the Scriptures and by the Spirit. Congregations, undergoing change, will learn to make unique mission-oriented decisions in relation to particular circumstances. They will grow in spiritual discernment for the actions they must take in response to the needs around them. Only in this way are falsehoods from the pervading culture increasingly revealed and stripped away.

Congregations undergoing such change are then also open to what some have called, a "decolonization" of the church. This term expresses that a significant element in what constitutes being a church is ethnically

---

17. Eph 6:18; John 4:23–24.

cultural, yet assumed normative, and therefore unreceptive to cultures other than the dominant culture of a denomination; therefore decolonization is necessary. I pastored an African American church for almost three decades on Chicago's south side. This congregation was related to a predominantly white denomination. Over the years, we made many changes to our worship life and ways of doing ministry. We also made various changes to the model constitution of our denomination. We simply made our constitution fit the way we actually constituted ourselves. It was later that I discovered that changes we made regarding reception of new members were changes to that part of the constitution our denomination deemed unchangeable. We made changes that fit the concrete reality of the congregation. Our hope is that such changes at the level of congregations will effect the openness and broadening of a denomination's documents and programs, and that barriers to mission are eradicated.

FOLLOWERS ARE SENT

> After this the Lord appointed seventy others and sent them on ahead of him in pairs to every town and place where he himself intended to go."[18]

Within the community, which Jesus gathers, training takes place for being sent out into the world to do the work of God's reign. Within Jesus' community, followers learn what they could only learn in relation to one another: how to love when one sins against you, how far forgiveness goes, how to be great under God's reign as servants to others, how to respond to denier and traitor, how to do kingdom work together (as two or three or twelve or seventy), what to expect from authorities (opposition), how to handle suffering, how to deal with death, how to suffer with others, how to pray, how to minister healing, how to recognize and be led by the Spirit, and how to proclaim God's reign.

Consider who made up Jesus' band of followers: Peter (who later denied knowing Jesus), James, and John, all fishermen; Matthew, a national traitor (having collected taxes for the occupying power of Rome); Thomas, who struggled with believing and yet spoke of going to Jerusalem to die with Jesus; Judas, who betrayed Jesus; Simon, a revolutionary (zealot); Mary Magdalene, from whom Jesus had cast out seven demons; Joanna, the wife of King Herod's household manager, Chuza; Salome, who bought spices for Jesus' burial; Mary (the mother of James), who with Mary Magdalene,

---

18. Luke 10:1.

Joanna, Salome, and other women went to the tomb to prepare Jesus' body for burial. This sampling of followers gives us a sense of the diversity. It was a cross-section of society. We also recognize varying degrees of commitment and the variety of struggles experienced by those who followed Jesus. As we read in the Gospels about the interaction between Jesus and his followers, we also see the varying kinds of instruction Jesus gives, depending on situation and individual disciple.

I reflect on the diversity in the church I served on Chicago's southside. I think of the rich community prayer time, on Sunday mornings, following the sermon and song. Often, during prayer, need met words of grace. People shared their struggles, experienced healing and, at times, experienced prophetic words, by which they heard God speak to their situations. I imagine Jesus praying with his followers and addressing their specific needs—challenging, comforting, and encouraging them. Within the community, Jesus' followers experienced his ministry. That ministry continues with the risen Jesus among God's gathered people.

In their worship, their singing hymns, receiving instruction, and nurturing their relationships with one another, Jesus' disciples were being prepared for going out into the world. Jesus modeled for them the ministry he was sending them to do and then gave them authority for that ministry, sending them in the power of the same Spirit that empowered him. As he did the work of God's reign, he was, at the same time, mentoring his followers. On one occasion, those disciples who were unable to cast out an evil spirit, received direction from Jesus: "This kind can come out only through prayer." They would have to go deeper in prayer.[19] On another occasion, when they thought it was their job to send away children so Jesus would not be bothered, he told them to let the children come to him, for it is "to such as these that the kingdom of heaven belongs."[20] Jesus was model and mentor.

Above all, Jesus made it clear who were his family: "Who is my mother, and who are my brothers?" And pointing to his disciples, he said, "Here are my mother and my brothers! For whoever does the will of my Father in heaven is my brother and sister and mother."[21] Jesus gathers together true community, the children of God who are sent out to do the will of God. And God's will for them was to "cure the sick . . . and say to them, 'The kingdom of God has come near to you.'"[22]

---

19. Mark 9:29.
20. Matt 19:14.
21. Matt 12:49–50.
22. Luke 10:1–12.

This continues to be the kind of community Jesus calls forth. We, who are followers, are sent into a broken, needy world where the deepest human desire and need is for the source of life and love. We are to proclaim the nearness of the source and call people to return to it—to turn from idols to serve the true and living God. We are to respond to the needs around us. Like the "good Samaritan," we must refuse to walk around the wounded person, but rather bind up the wounds, bringing healing and restoration. Jesus sends his followers where people are hurting and in need; he sends them into places of breakdown and despair, to bring hope and new life. Jesus is a model for the response his followers are to have toward the oppressive systems and forces around them. Like Jesus, they are to confront and address the unjust power of the Herods, Pilates, and Pharisees of the world who "tie up heavy burdens, hard to bear, and lay them on the shoulders of others; but they themselves are unwilling to lift a finger to move them."[23]

If we are not doing this kind of work as communities of faith, something has gone wrong. If we do little more than look for other "church people" to join our church, we have lost our way, and we are living distant from Jesus and his leading. If we simply gauge the internal desires of "our" church as a way of deciding what to do, we have forgotten the Holy Spirit.

Many churches of our time are like Jesus' hometown of Nazareth where "he could do no deed of power there, except that he laid his hands on a few sick people and cured them." Mark tells us that Jesus "was amazed at their unbelief."[24] Jesus apparently quotes a proverb when he says, "Prophets are not without honor, except in their hometown, and among their own kin, and in their own house." For many church-goers, familiarity with Jesus robs them of the ability to take Jesus seriously enough to follow him. They have theologies that they are comfortable with, confessions and creeds that they can easily and glibly repeat and familiar hymns that they enjoy singing. As with Jesus' hometown neighbors, they easily talk about Jesus as if they knew him. However, the truth is that they may simply have become comfortable with a caricature of Jesus that fits easily with their life-styles. Jesus is, for them, a symbol of God's acceptance, but not of God's liberation. There is little challenge to their values and priorities and little change.

What is needed is reality, not familiarity. We need the truth that disturbs our false ways, disturbs our false images of Jesus and disturbs our comfort with false ways. I have found that I have had to keep coming back to the Jesus of the Gospels, receive afresh the witness to him and his teaching. I have to let Jesus continually break up my false conceptions of him, let myself

23. Matt 23:4.
24. Mark 6:1–6.

be disturbed by his teaching and hear again his call upon my life. And trust him enough to follow where he leads.

So, how do we, who are familiar with Jesus and risk taking him for granted, hear a fresh call to follow? How do we come out of our denial concerning our condition? If we are relatively comfortable and satisfied with our familiar Jesus, how do we meet the real Jesus—the one who liberates and transforms lives, who takes some fishermen and makes them fish for people?

In the story of Jesus and his hometown, following the words, "He could do no deed of power there," is this phrase: "except that he laid his hands on a few sick people and cured them." There were a few people in Nazareth who got beyond their familiarity with him. What happened to them, which did not happen to the others?

Often, it is when everything is breaking down, when we feel helpless, when we know we are in need of help beyond anything we can do for ourselves, that we start truly reaching out. Those addicted to drugs talk about hitting rock bottom—and at that point seeking help. I imagine that, for those few who were healed in Nazareth, their need made them reach out to Jesus for the possibility of help. From a place of need, no longer able to help themselves, came the beginnings of hope and a willingness to turn to Jesus for what he had to give.

But what if we do not experience or recognize ourselves as needy—at least not so needy that we must undergo change? What if we are relatively satisfied with our lives? We are self-satisfied, and Jesus is somewhere in the mix, but it is a "familiar" Jesus from whom we expect little change in our lives. How, then, is the change to come?

For addicts who have been in denial about their condition, telling themselves that they are doing fine, there is something called "intervention." Family and friends gather around them and share with them the impact of their addiction upon their lives. They share their pain, their loss of a relationship with their loved one, and their hurt. They share, with a plan in place and a way forward for their loved one; a bed is ready at a treatment center and steps for their loved one to take are clearly outlined, as well as the consequences if the person does not take the steps. The person's family will no longer be enablers.

Something like that has to happen for us in our self-satisfaction and our false familiarity with Jesus. Jesus does interventions. He speaks to our condition. If we have operated as if it were up to us to secure our lives, Jesus speaks truth to the idolatry of our security: "For those who want to save their life will lose it, and those who lose their life for my sake, and for the sake of the gospel, will save it." In other words, let go of trying to secure your life the way you think you want it to be. Lose your life: Give it up for the sake of the good news of God's reign. Let God reign in your life so that you walk by faith and in obedience to God's will.

With words such as these, Jesus does interventions. Jesus' words disturb our lethargy, complacency, and the denial of our condition. At times, the words are brutally cutting in their truth ("Woe to you, scribes and Pharisees, hypocrites!"). The truth of such words are meant to shake those being addressed out of their denial and self-deceit. The words are meant to cut through cover-ups, to reveal the need, brokenness, and false dependencies. Such words are directed to deliverance from bondage to idols, so that we may be healed and restored in our relationship with God and others. Letting Jesus speak a fresh word to us through the Gospels by submitting to his words in obedience becomes an intervention.

Healthy congregations, as they embody Christ, are places where interventions take place. Where needy people experience deliverance from false dependencies, there is a community that does loving interventions. Just as recovering addicts go find other addicts and, knowing the signs of deception and denial, can speak truth and know the spiritual journey that is necessary for healing, so spiritually liberated communities of faith can do the same. They are truly places of healing.

On the other hand, a church satisfied with a falsely familiar Jesus, who does little in the way of interventions, leaves members with their false-dependencies, no longer calling them to turn from idols to their source. Such a church has little to offer others who are in bondage and denial. Of course, pastors and leaders are particularly important for there to be change in churches. Prayerful leadership is needed, dependent on God, open to the Spirit, willing to overturn tables and risk losing members. The word of truth has to again go forth. By the truth people are set free.

For change, people again must realize their deepest desire for the source of their lives: a God not of their own making, but the One who remains mystery, who cannot be defined and controlled by us, but who releases us to be our true selves. From that desire, decisions are made: the decision to turn, to receive God's reign, to say "yes" to God and to follow Jesus, God's Anointed. Then, participating in Jesus' faithful obedience, people must take one step after another, learning to discern God's call, responding to the Spirit of God. Following.

Since our desires and decisions have become misplaced, hard truth must be proclaimed in love. The idols in our lives must be addressed: our idolatry of power, pleasure, possessions, comfort, and convenience. Our idolatry of race, clan, nation, and national security must be unmasked. The symptoms of our idolatry often must be described in order for us to move past our denials. When we are disturbed by the truth, we must be encouraged to be steadfast hearers of the word. We must realize that push-back from our idolatrous condition is to be expected. We have to press forward in hearing and doing the truth. As more is revealed, we must keep turning from false dependencies, so that God's reign can claim more of our lives.

In congregations undergoing change, leaders and proclaimers must expect rejection. There will be those who leave the church, like the rich young man who turned away from Jesus when told to give away his idol of wealth to the poor and come and follow. There will be those who, hearing the word addressing the idolatry of nation or race, threaten to leave, because they do not want "politics" in sermons. Their decision to leave notwithstanding, the word still must go forth. We are to be witnesses to God's governance and no other.

The point is this: For established congregations that are turned inward, the risen Jesus is present with the same fundamental message: "Repent for the reign of God is near." Turn from idols. Return to the Lord your God. It is a call for response. It speaks to our desire and decision-making, without which there is no following and no going out into the world with good news. Those who are being liberated from idols and experiencing the freedom of the children of God go out to spread the good news. The ministry of word and Spirit, by its very nature, turns people around and moves them out. For people of faith, this becomes the journey of their lives.

Not going out, for members of a congregation, is a symptom of spiritual breakdown. When there is little or no testimony of God's good news out in the world, little or no sharing of hope, little doing justice or concretely showing mercy, and little faithfulness to the sending that God does, a profound spiritual need exists that must be addressed. If the neediness stems from despair, the word of hope in Christ must be declared; if from self-satisfaction and lethargy, the call to repent from false dependencies must be declared.

Jesus gathers followers to send them out. Where there is no going, it is because there is no following. Following other allegiances instead of following Jesus into God's reign must call for repentance. When God reigns, it is difficult to remain attached to, and be bound by, other gods.

By following Jesus, communities of faith shed a false Christianity. Together, we gain clarity for what truly matters. We gain commitment to God's will; we desire to know it, in order to do it. We begin to embody the Christ reality, so that the world can get a view of what is on the heart of God and what love in action looks like. We leave aside ourselves and "our religion." We need not spend much energy defending ourselves against the world, since we are being energized for going out into the world. We are servants shedding light on that which is not of God and, even more important, bringing to fruition that which comes from God. In our gatherings, we share hope for the liberation of humanity in Christ.

When we move out from our gatherings, we expect God to use us. We expect to be instruments of deliverance from the power of sin and liberation from oppression. We expect others to come alive through the power of God and for justice to "roll down like waters." We expect that there will be those who reject what we bring and who will fight against it. We understand this dynamic, because we experience it in ourselves as well. We know, however, that just as God frees us—we who have resisted (and experience a condition of resistance)—and turns us around (and keeps turning us around), so God can do that for others. We now have become witnesses to God's grace.

WITNESSES

> But you will receive power when the Holy Spirit has come upon you; and you will be my witnesses in Jerusalem, in all Judea and Samaria, and to the ends of the earth.[25]

Previously, we may have been witnesses to various "good things" that have happened in our lives, even finding personal glory in some of those things. They may have made us look good in the eyes of others, or so we thought. We witnessed to that which we cared about, or to which we were committed. Although we went to church, we rarely brought God into our ordinary conversations or witnessed to justice and mercy by words and actions. We may have kept ourselves distant from those who were actively doing the work of justice. We may have avoided those who were actively calling others back to God and encouraging them to believe that God is near and can be found. That was not our life, not who we were.

But now we have returned to the source of our lives, to the Lover of our souls; we have a radically new witness. We have been liberated to share with others the goodness of God and to do the work of making right what is wrong around us. We witness to God's mercy, justice, and faithfulness. We witness to where security, identity, and fulfillment is found.

The story of Acts is the story of Jesus' followers, filled with the Spirit, witnessing to Jesus. They operated as those being sent out. They went to temple and synagogue and then moved beyond Judea to other nations. They proclaimed God's action: The man Jesus, anointed by God, from God, having the imprint of God's being, died for our liberation and was raised for

25. Acts 1:8.

our victory over sin and death. Therefore, they called others to turn to God, receive forgiveness and new life in the Spirit. They proclaimed a message and demonstrated the power of what they proclaimed in a ministry of healing and deliverance from evil.

Their activity bore fruit in that many turned to God and became participants of the divine nature through Jesus, *the* Participant of the divine nature. Communities of Jesus' followers were formed; these were house gatherings where believers experienced life in the Spirit and heard God's call that sent them out to tell the story to others.

This movement, which brought new life to many, also created disturbance to the present order. The kingdom of God being ushered in was very different from the established kingdoms of the world. The power of God, which was a power of justice and life, clashed with the power of oppression and death. People were being released from their fear of the various powers, earthly and heavenly, human and cosmic. "God put this power to work in Christ when he raised him from the dead and seated him at his right hand in the heavenly places, far above all rule and authority and power and dominion, and above every name that is named, not only in this age but also in the age to come."[26] Caesar was no longer lord, the gods were figments of human imagination; the various spirits and demons lost their power.

The disruption that God's reign caused met opposition from the various "authorities" of the present order. Followers experienced the same kind of opposition that Jesus experienced, but also his joy in God and his willingness to do the work of his Father. They became, like Jesus, a "sign that is opposed." Where Christians today walk this same walk, they continue to be a sign that is opposed.

However, where Christians have aligned themselves to political parties and ideologies, or have become enamored by earthly power as a way to carve out a place for themselves in the present order, they have ceased to witness to and be a sign of God's reign. They have become ideological organisms aligned with earthly power for their own gain. Jesus' words remain: "If you seek to gain your life, you will lose it." You will lose both life and witness.

True gatherings of Jesus' followers are learning to live from their source. From a fellowship of worship and prayer, they move out with power to declare what God is doing and what is on the heart of God for humanity. They give witness against the powers of oppression and death, sin and breakdown. They become instruments of God's healing and deliverance, justice and mercy. Their witness and their following demand their daily dying that they might daily rise to their mission.

---

26. Eph 1:20–21.

7

Following the Crucified and Risen One

Walter Altmann, in his book, *Luther and Liberation*, points out that for Martin Luther, "the new life of those redeemed by Christ will take the same shape as his life." Altmann notes that Luther replaced the notion of the "imitation of Christ" with that of being "'con-formed' with Christ, to take on the same form as Christ."[1] This means:

> Free from bondage, free from sin, death, and the curse, the new life is expressed in accordance with the cross of Christ, in the same downward movement of God's love to the depth of evil and suffering, in the same emptying of mercy, in the same carrying of heavy burdens, in shared loneliness. To suffer, according to Luther, is the royal attire of the Christian. Now, conformation in the cross; in the end, conformation in glory.[2]

The roots for Luther's notion of conformation are found in Paul, for whom participation in the Christ reality, the being united to Christ's dying and rising, are central. In taking on the same form of Christ by being "in Christ," we become, as with Jesus, signs that are opposed by the world. Our congregations become gatherings of "sent ones," witnesses, agitators; we are vessels of divine love and therefore of liberation and healing. Rather than merely an external attempt to live up to the example of Jesus, Christ is being formed in us, as Christ abides in us. Following the Crucified One has an inward reality. We are being conformed to Christ's self-emptying and cross-carrying. However, we also get a taste of the glory yet to come, in our experiences of

1. Altmann, *Luther and Liberation*, 60–61.
2. Altmann, *Luther and Liberation*, 60–61.

resurrection victory over that which has had us enslaved. The Risen Christ is experienced in our being empowered to serve others, with the authority for action that we receive from God.

In what follows, we will meditate on the meaning of following Jesus as the Crucified and Risen One, as we are being conformed to him through participating in the reality of the one who is "the same yesterday and today and forever."[3]

FOLLOWING THE CRUCIFIED ONE

> The cross is a paradoxical religious symbol because it inverts the world's value system with the news that hope comes by way of defeat, that suffering and death do not have the last word, that the last shall be first and the first last. (James H. Cone, *The Cross and the Lynching Tree*)[4]
>
> God does not reveal Godself in full glory, but in and through the infinite poverty and weakness of human nature. Christ has shown that the way to God passes through human poverty, precariousness, vulnerability, and weakness. (Jean-Pierre Fortin, *Grace in Auschwitz; A Holocaust Christology*)[5]
>
> On the slave ships the moan became the language of stolen strangers, the articulation of unspeakable fears, the precursor to joy yet unknown. The moan is the birthing sound, the first movement toward a creative response to oppression, the entry into the heart of contemplation through the crucible of crisis. (Barbara A. Holmes, *Joy Unspeakable: Contemplative Practices of the Black Church*)[6]
>
> Jesus cried with a loud voice, "Eli, Eli, lema sabachthani?" that is, "My God, my God, why have you forsaken me?" (Matt 27:46)
>
> Then Jesus, crying with a loud voice, said, "Father, into your hands I commend my spirit." Having said this, he breathed his last. (Luke 23:46)

Approximately one-third of each of the four Gospels is devoted to the suffering and death of Jesus. Clearly, Jesus being brought before the authorities, his trials, his beatings, and his crucifixion are central to the "good news"

---

3. Heb 13:8.
4. Cone, *The Cross and the Lynching Tree*, 309, Kindle.
5 Fortin, *Grace in Auschwitz; A Holocaust Christology*, 157
6. Holmes, *Joy Unspeakable*, chapter 3, section 7, Kindle.

message of these writings. They remain central to followers of Jesus today. We follow the Crucified One.

With his crucifixion, Jesus plunges into the darkness, entering fully into this world's suffering and its source in evil (that is, in the power of death). Jesus experiences the loss of what ought to be: the death of love. He feels the depth of this emptying and dehumanization: "My God, my God, why have you forsaken me." He enters into the darkness that has produced Auschwitz, the Middle Passage, Hiroshima and Nagasaki, enslavement, genocide, torture, brutality, and war—all of which are manifestations of the power of death, of spiritual death. Jesus had prophesied his death as a liberation for many and viewed it as his final act, that act which he had been called by God to undergo. His life was not simply taken from him: he gave it up in response to God's call for the liberation of the world.[7]

Early followers of Jesus strained to put the meaning of this event into words. Paul puts it starkly: "God made him to be sin."[8] Christ, "who knew no sin," became identified with sin and evil. He took on our identity, our loss of being, our inhumanity and dehumanizing ways. In 1 Peter, we are told that Jesus "bore our sins in his body on the cross, so that, free from sins, we might live for righteousness; by his wounds you have been healed."[9] We stand before a mystery. This man, Jesus, sent from God, God's Anointed, enters into our spiritual death. He takes our sin upon himself, takes our brokenness, suffering, and death, so that we may be healed. Through this human being, healing comes to all humanity.

Paul sees this mystery in the experience of baptism. Through baptism, we are united to Christ and we participate in his death and resurrection. In Christ, we die and are raised to "newness of life."[10] The baptismal image of going under the water is a symbol of dying; the rising out of the water, a symbol of our being raised from the dead. From being dead toward God and our true selves, we are released alive to God and our true selves. Paul writes, "We know that our old self was crucified with him so that the body of sin might be destroyed, and we might no longer be enslaved to sin. For whoever has died is freed from sin. But if we have died with Christ, we believe that we will also live with him."[11]

---

7. Mark 10:45; John 6:51.

8. "For our sake [God] made him to be sin who knew no sin, so that in him we might become the righteousness of God" (2 Cor 5:21).

9. 1 Pet 2:24.

10. Rom 6:3–4.

11. Rom 6:6–9.

In the Anointed Jesus, we find our true humanity and relationship with God.[12] God is at work in Christ so that, as we participate in Christ, we become the human beings God created us to be. As Paul puts it, "In Christ God was reconciling the world to himself, not counting their trespasses against them."[13] God, in Christ, enters into our suffering. Jesus, God's Anointed, is "the image of the invisible God,"[14] the Offspring and Expression of God.[15] In this union of God and humanity, Jesus is God's revelation in the flesh—God manifest in our humanity. God is united with us, our history, and our suffering. Some have written in stark, bold terms of the "Crucified God" as a way of acknowledging God's presence in our suffering, need, and vulnerability.[16] Above all, God is the source and action of our healing through the crucified Christ made real by the activity of the Spirit of God in our lives.

When we follow the Crucified One, we enter into this reality of God's presence with suffering people and are a part of God's action in bringing deliverance and new life by the power of God's Spirit. There is no ministry of healing and liberation without entering into the suffering of the world—acknowledging our own suffering and sharing with others who hurt. Therefore, Jesus says we must take up our cross. Following the Crucified One means a particular relationship with suffering, death, and the sin that causes suffering. Following Jesus changes the way we relate to sin, suffering, and death.

OUR CHANGING RELATIONSHIP TO SIN

> "The death he died, he died to sin, once for all; but the life he lives, he lives to God. So you also must consider yourselves dead to sin and alive to God in Christ Jesus." [17]

Paul often uses the word "sin" as an aspect of the human condition—the condition of idolatry. It is to this condition, this old self, a self turned inward upon itself, that Christ died. We, who have come to participate in Christ's death, in union with Christ, must now view this old self as crucified, setting us free to be alive to God. It is not that this condition of idolatry simply goes away. In a sense, we experience ourselves in two worlds with two

---

12. He is the New Adam through whom we are released from the Old Adam (humanity in its bondage to sin and the power of death). Rom 5:12–15; 1 Cor 15:21–23, 45.

13. 2 Cor 5:19.

14. Col 1:15.

15. John 1:1–4, 14.

16. Moltmann, *The Crucified God*.

17. Rom 6:10–11.

diametrically opposed conditions. As we grow in Christ, we grow in the experience of our freedom, sin no longer having the *same* power over us. And yet we continue to experience its power and its conflict with the new life. At times, it may seem that sin's power remains quite alive and the new life minimal. Growth of the new self feels slow. Others may notice our growth before we do. The new life is "hidden with Christ in God"[18] and it grows as we grow in Christ, dying with Christ to the idolatrous self that unrelentingly continues its attempts to make itself source and center.

Consider the ways this happens, as we follow the Crucified One. As the false self (the idolatrous self) gives way to the true self, our idolatry of pleasure, possessions, power, race, nation, technology, and so on, dies. It is a daily dying, as we follow the one whose life was a "daily dying" to the ways of an idolatrous world. Jesus' daily dying is alluded to in the Gospels when they provide us with a story of temptation. In this story, Jesus turns away from the idolatry of physical needs and of trying to manipulate God rather than trust God. He turns from trying to center life in the powers and ways of the idolatrous systems of the world.[19] We further see the turning away, the dying, when Jesus, tempted by Peter from taking up his cross, says to him, "Get behind me, Satan!"[20] We see Jesus commit himself to the journey and calling God has for him, dying to anything that would get in the way. The one who tells us to take up our cross daily, takes up *his* cross daily. And we are to follow him.

The Crucified One, whom we follow, is being formed in us. His daily dying to sin becomes our daily dying. That is why Paul tells us we "must consider [ourselves] dead to sin and alive to God in Christ Jesus." Being "in Christ" and following Jesus places our focus now on Christ and on what God is doing through Christ. Our focus is not on this or that particular sin, as if the way forward were to daily identify individual sins and work on ridding ourselves of them. When we try, we fail miserably. If we delude ourselves that we are making progress by this legalistic manner, we only gain self-righteousness, hypocrisy, and self-deceit.

Followers of the Crucified One must consider themselves dead to sin, not because we no longer experience the power of sin or no longer have to contend with sin, but because we now contend with sin "in Christ," in whom the victory has already been won. In Christ, we are liberated children of God, alive to God. Therefore, our focus must be to grow in Christ. "Abide in me," Jesus tells us in the Gospel of John. "Without me you can do nothing."

18. Col 3:3.
19. Matt 4:1–11.
20. Matt 16:22–24.

We walk by faith, not by the sight of all the brokenness of our lives. By faith, we follow Jesus into the new life—the life in Christ—and become alive to the will of God.

We experience confession and repentance in relation to individual sins, but that experience has to do with the Holy Spirit at work in us: convicting, freeing, opening our eyes to the ways in which we are to walk and empowering us for the steps we are to take. The movement forward is not left to our own resources, but has to do with our life *in Christ*. And in this life, we live under God's mercy. Forgiveness and mercy free us from thinking we must work on this sin and that sin, in and of ourselves. Therefore, we are free to turn our focus on what God is doing in and among us and in this world where we are called to be salt, light, and yeast, by the grace of God. We are free to be led by the Spirit of God.

Our relationship to sin has changed in Christ. Sin is no longer our problem, in so far as it would make us either despairing and despondent, or self-righteous and judgmental. We are freed to be witnesses to the new life in Christ, through whom we have been made alive to God and to God's will. Now, our focus is on living out God's purpose and witnessing to what is on the heart of God for humanity, as we are coming to know it. We are freed to work for change, to do justice, love mercy, and live faithfully.

OUR CHANGING RELATIONSHIP TO SUFFERING

If we could avoid suffering we would. We generally do not seek it, unless something has gone wrong with a healthy sense of self. Suffering usually comes unannounced and is relatively beyond our control. Some suffering is the result of our bad decisions, the consequences of which we often can do little to change. Other troubles and trials come from the actions of others or from the happenstances of life: an auto accident, sickness, natural catastrophe, loss of loved ones, loss of a job, breakdown in relationships or in society, and so on. When these things happen, we are comparatively passive participants, in the sense that we now must undergo, or suffer through, what is happening to us. At times, there is little we can do but "accept the things we cannot change." That is, we must take up our cross and move forward. Humanly speaking, Jesus had little choice but to go where his adversaries took him, once they had control, through trial and beating and crucifixion. The risen Jesus indicated the same experience would be Peter's, "When you grow old, you will stretch out your hands, and someone else will fasten a belt around you and take you where you do not wish to go."[21] Peter would walk

21. John 21:18.

the same road as the one he was following. We are told that these words indicated how Peter would die. Jesus then says to him, "Follow me." Follow me, in patient endurance, when someone takes you where you do not wish to go.

When suffering comes, then generally "taking up the cross"—that is, taking up our suffering—is the healthy choice. Various forms of escape may present themselves, but they are temporary, and often add to the suffering. When experiencing emotional pain or depression, we may seek the cover of alcohol, but eventually we will become sober and add a hangover to our pain. We can try to lose ourselves in other addictions that, because of our dependence on them, act like a drug: social media, shopping, eating, internet, sex, and so on. This does not mean that there is no place for taking pain medicine, for example, to relieve physical pain. But we still must deal with the cause of the pain.

Suffering is about enduring what has befallen us. In order to change the things we can, we must accept what we cannot change, which means suffering the trial or difficulty. We go on with life and do what is necessary by walking through the pain. When my younger brother died of leukemia, as my mother shared later, she no longer wanted to live. But she had four other children that needed her and she had to go on for their sake. She could not simply run from the pain, seeking escape into inactivity, sleep, or self-medication. She took up her suffering and lovingly addressed the needs of her other children. Taking up the cross that comes to us becomes a way of life that *gives* life.

There is, however, another aspect to Jesus' call to take up our crosses. There is a cross that comes with following Jesus, a cross that we would not experience if it were not for our following. This was briefly addressed in chapter 3. Here, we make some further observations and recognize the significance of Christ being formed in us, to undergo this cross-bearing.

We know little of Jesus' early life. Mark tells us that the people of his hometown knew Jesus as a carpenter. They may have known him as a teacher as well. We do not know what form suffering took in those days, but we can assume he endured the daily trials that are inherent to our humanity. Carpenters are not without a "cross," nor are teachers. However, it is the period in which he proclaimed God's reign and healed people that the Gospels provide some of the contours of his cross. Before his passion, he was learning to endure the various trials that came his way as he lived, in obedience to his Father's will, to proclaim God's reign.

He immersed himself in the crowds of people who "were harassed and helpless, like sheep without a shepherd." Out of compassion (which means "to suffer with"), Jesus entered into their struggles, reaching out to heal and to share the good news of God's reign. He felt the weight of this work, saying to his followers, "The harvest is plentiful, but the laborers are few; therefore ask the Lord of the harvest to send out laborers into his harvest."[22] At times, he sought relief by going to a place of solitude to pray.[23] Furthermore, his engagement with his followers brought its own cross as he endured their lack of faith and understanding, causing him to lash out at them, "You faithless generation, how much longer must I be among you? How much longer must I put up with you?"[24] We recognize some of the crosses Jesus bore before the cross on which he was crucified. His ministry to people came with a cross—as does ours.

And then there was the cross of opposition. "The Pharisees went out and conspired against him, how to destroy him."[25] The Pharisees also relayed the message to Jesus that "Herod wants to kill you."[26] And Jesus warns his followers, "Watch out—beware of the yeast of the Pharisees and the yeast of Herod."[27] The opposition—Jewish and Roman—led to Jesus' crucifixion.

Jesus did not live in a world essentially different from ours. There is one human race and one human history, and Christ, the image and Word of God, entered it. Jesus, the Christ, lived his life and mission in the midst of worldly power. The way power operated in Jerusalem and Rome was not so different, in its essentials, from the way it operates in Washington D.C. today, in any of the world's centers of power or, for that matter, in the boardrooms of transnational corporations. As significant as democracy is, it does not change the dynamic of our condition in sin. "We the people" choose leaders that will ensure that, as a nation, we will be capable of dominating other nations as necessary to maintain our "exceptional" (and super-power) status, security, and leverage. We the people have built and maintain, at great expense, the means to coerce others by way of a massive military and sophisticated weaponry, which we frequently use.

In this world, with its power dynamics, Jesus comes proclaiming a very different kind of power and governance in the reign of God. Unlike the way worldly power operates to obtain advantage over others, to "lord it over them," Jesus makes it clear that this must not be the way of his followers who are called to be servants to one another. "For the Son of Man came not to be served but to serve, and to give his life a ransom for many."[28]

---

22. Matt 9:35–38.
23. Luke 5:16.
24. Mark 9:19.
25. Matt 12:14.
26. Luke 13:31.
27. Mark 8:15.
28. Mark 10:42–45.

Jesus' followers are to operate among themselves in a very different manner from that of the nations of the world. And they are to witness to a radically different reality in word and practice. They are to live from the power that serves in love. In their relationships and their witness, Jesus' followers confront the dynamics of egotism, pride, and arrogance, as are manifest in the power-plays between individuals, groups, and nations. This clearly becomes a significant aspect of the cross they carry.

As servants, following Jesus, Christ being formed in us, we are being made responsive to needy people, who like ourselves, need God and what God gives. We come as servants with the healing and deliverance that we have received from God. We are learning to view ourselves as sent—especially to those carrying heavy burdens. We are sent with hope for those who live under the weight of injustice and oppression. We come against those who add to the burdens and we work to make right what is wrong. We bring the good news of God's nearness to individuals and of God's work that frees us. At the same time, we work to bring change to the environment in which individuals and their families live. This work is both calling and cross. It is action that flows from the obedience of following; and it endures struggle and, at times, great disturbances and trials.

Followers of Jesus are to be engaged in the world as witnesses. We are not called to condemn, for we would come under the same judgment, given our own prideful, arrogant ways. But, as we follow Jesus and as Christ is formed in us, freeing us to serve in love, we must witness to the new way of being that we are discovering. We cannot, for example, simply align ourselves to a particular political party or ideology. The reign of God critiques all ideologies. Our allegiance is to God's reign in Christ.

Furthermore, while still entangled in the power dynamics of our societies (they are inescapable), we cannot simply endorse or cooperate with those dynamics. Often our witness will be a protest. Our lives and witness will be a sign that contradicts the ways of our nation and world. When we are no longer such a sign, we have either stopped following or cordoned off (often unconsciously) the areas where we will follow and the areas we will not. We may make our personal relationships (and issues of responsibility, honesty, or sexual ethics) the focus of our following, while practicing a different set of values in business, social organizations, and nation. And yet, we are called to follow in every aspect of life. We are to take up our cross and follow, not avoiding the struggle.

We who are followers of Jesus are being changed as we follow. The key to following is our being "in Christ." The good news is that this Christ reality in which we participate is the reality of our one humanity, one history, and one world. Jesus, the Christ, lived his life within the same dynamics of the world that we experience today. That lived reality becomes ours in our union with Christ. Jesus is not merely an external example for us, but comes to be formed in us as the Crucified and Risen Christ. As we become conformed to Christ, we become unable to be comfortable with the ways of this world. Our cross is formed as we become our true selves in Christ. We come to share in Jesus' faithful witness in the same world in which he lived.

In the book of Revelation, John is given a prophetic word that addresses the "seven churches that are in Asia." It is a word that encourages the church in the midst of persecution. His message comes "from Jesus Christ, the faithful witness, the firstborn of the dead, and the ruler of the kings of the earth."[29] As faithful witness, Jesus took up his cross and was obedient unto death. As "firstborn of the dead," he is our older brother who has opened up the way to new life. As "ruler of the kings of the earth," he brings in God's reign which has the final judgment over the decisions and actions of the world's leaders and the ways of the nations. Followers of Jesus receive encouragement in these words, as they seek to be faithful witnesses. John, who declares this message, views himself as a brother who shares with the churches in Jesus "the persecution and the kingdom and the patient endurance." What John suffered in exile on the island of Patmos, he shares not only with the sisters and brothers in Asia, but with all who patiently endure their crosses.

John's words give us a glimpse of the experience of the followers of Jesus in every time and place. How could the experience be any different, given the ways of the nations of the world? The dynamics of sin and evil have not changed with time. The depth of the suffering and endurance may change from age to age and place to place, but every follower of Jesus experiences a cross as they look forward to the breaking of "a yet more glorious day." The fourth verse of the hymn, "For All the Saints," expresses this reality: "And when the strife is fierce, the warfare long, steals on the ear the distant triumph song, and hearts are brave again, and arms are strong." We are emboldened for walking in the way of the Crucified One by the hope that is ours in the Risen One.

OUR CHANGING RELATIONSHIP TO DEATH

As was mentioned in chapter 3, the dying that we do on this journey of faith is a losing of our lives for Christ's sake and the gospel. It is a dying to a way of operating that is alienated from God. As we lose our lives to God, we receive our true selves, our true calling, and our cross. We add to those reflections a meditation on Jesus' dying, a dying that becomes ours "in Christ."

29. Rev 1:4–5.

Jesus' death is a very human one. The "seven last words of Christ"—meditated upon by Christians over the centuries—are revealing. As with other human beings who die with family and friends around, Jesus' death involved relationships. From the cross, he gave the care of his mother to his disciple, John. To his mother he said, "Woman, here is your son," and to John, "Here is your mother."[30] A man dying on a cross next to Jesus, asked of him, "Remember me when you come into your kingdom." (An unusual request from another dying man!) Jesus responded, "Truly I tell you, today you will be with me in Paradise."[31] As with others when dying, Jesus shared his needs with those surrounding him, "I am thirsty."[32] And he prayed for those who had put him on the cross and who were now taunting him, "Father, forgive them; for they do not know what they are doing."[33] Forgiveness of others is a human aspect of dying—a letting go of past hurts.

Jesus' relationship with God forms the center point of his dying. He cried out to God in his distress, "My God, my God, why have you forsaken me?"[34] He addressed God with his feelings of being abandoned by God. Who else could he turn to in the depths of despair? He had taken up the cross God had given him and he was experiencing its profound dehumanization. And so he cried out, "My God, My God." As his earthly calling and cross came to an end, he said, "It is finished," and "Father, into your hands I commend my spirit."[35] It is a cry of trust in the midst of the darkness.

The Crucified One died our death. Emptying himself, and without having anything to prop him up, feeling forsaken, he trusted his life to God. His dying becomes ours. As we follow Jesus, allowing his dying to take form in us, we are enabled to take up our own dying—we who have lived in denial of death. Ernest Becker, in his book, *The Denial of Death*, wrote of our fundamental problem: the denial of being mortal.[36] We prefer to act as if we are the creator of our own existence, rather than a mortal creature. We act as though our life is in our own hands. It is in reference to this way of acting that James writes when he says, "Come now, you who say, 'Today or tomorrow we will go to such and such a town and spend a year there, doing business and making money.' Yet you do not even know what

---

30. John 19:26–27.
31. Luke 23:39–43.
32. John 19:28.
33. Luke 23:34.
34. Matt 27:45–46.
35. John 19:28; Luke 23:46.
36. Becker, *Denial of Death*.

tomorrow will bring. What is your life? For you are a mist that appears for a little while and then vanishes."[37]

By following Jesus, we learn how to die. We are released from our denial, from the lie by which we have attempted to live. We are freed to acknowledge our profound need for God, the source of our lives. In Jesus' faith in God, in his taking up his cross and calling, and emptying himself, his dying becomes ours. Through Anointed Jesus' death, our relationship to death is being changed. We, who have run from death, are now, in Christ, beginning to die daily so that we may also rise daily. We die to the denial of our creatureliness and embrace our true selves as they come from God. This kind of dying becomes a way of life.

Paul expresses this reality acutely: "I have been crucified with Christ and I no longer live, but Christ lives in me. And the life that I now live in my body, I live by faith, indeed, by the faithfulness of God's Son, who loved me and gave himself for me."[38] We die with the Messiah and share in his faith, so that what we are becoming is no longer attempted by our own efforts, but now comes as a life *given* to us, lived by faith in God through Messiah Jesus. And this life given is an act of love that now claims us.

We have come to recognize the futility of all our attempts to make something of ourselves. This includes our attempts to "better ourselves," or to live by a higher morality. Whatever moral law we have attempted to live by has been undone by our condition in sin (that is, by our idolatry of self). We have had to die to our attempts to morally rectify ourselves. Our condition simply undoes whatever we attempt, in and of ourselves. As Paul says, "The power of sin is the law." Our condition fights the restrictions of the law. (If you live in a glass house, do not put a sign out in front that says, "Do not throw stones.") Consequently, trying to live by a moral law has us caught up in hypocrisy and self-righteousness.

Liberation is found in the free gift of life lived from God, a life that is ours in Anointed Jesus. Dying to our condition in sin is a dying that is ours in the Anointed One, as we live in him. The primary focus is no longer on trying to better ourselves, but on growing in the new reality that is ours, in the Messiah, as God gives it to us. Our orientation is to the source of our lives. A branch draws its life from the tree and dies if cut off from the source of its life. Like a branch, we simply must abide in the source of our being, living by faith. And walking by faith. The Spirit of God now helps us to see our next steps, not only those steps that adhere to our general humanity, but

---

37. Jas 4:13–14.
38. Gal 2:19–20 CEB.

those that are specifically related to our individual callings. Our actions flow from their source in God.

What makes us fearful of dying, of self-emptying, is our condition in sin. We are afraid of losing the life we think we have been building. In this condition, we think that if we could simply have and manage God's salvation (whatever aspects we imagine are good for us) as an add-on, our self-idolatry could find a way to include it in what it is building. Jesus, however, tells us we must lose our *lives*. In our spiritually sick condition, we are fine with losing *part* of our lives, if we can choose the part, because that would enable us to continue to "play god." These ways of thinking are our old self, running scared. To this experience, Paul writes good news, "The sting of death is sin, and the power of sin is the law. But thanks be to God, who gives us the victory through our Lord Jesus Christ."[39]

RESURRECTION VICTORY THROUGH LAYING DOWN OUR LIVES

> I lay down my life in order to take it up again. No one takes it from me, but I lay it down of my own accord. I have power to lay it down, and I have power to take it up again.[40]

These words from the Gospel of John that portray Jesus laying down his life are words for us as well. Through the Anointed One, we also are to lay down our lives in order to take them up again. With Jesus, we are given power to lay down our lives and power to take our lives up again. The lives we take up are not the same as the lives that we laid down. The laying down of our lives has changed everything. The life we take up is no longer a life that operates as if it can live without its source. We have laid that life down. Our lives and our identity are in God. The false self (false, in that it has been an attempt to construct itself apart from God) is dying away and our true selves, as they come from God, are being raised up.

Paul writes dramatically about this: "Everything old has passed away; see, everything has become new."[41] Jesus calls this a being born from above—from the true source of our lives.[42] The Spirit draws us to this laying down of our lives, helps us to decide to lay down our lives and empowers us to take up the new life in God. This laying down of our lives is the foundational

39. 1 Cor 15:56–57.
40. John 10:17–18.
41. 2 Cor 5:17.
42. John 3:3.

act of our being. It carries us into a life in the Spirit, which is a life of laying down and raising up—daily. Follow daily; die daily; rise daily.

How else is there growth in loving and ministering to others? Jesus, the good shepherd, lays down his life in response to God's will and for the sake of "the sheep." We are to do the same. We lay down our lives in response to God and to God's will, and we are freed to take up our lives in serving one another. The life we give to God is also a giving of ourselves, for the sake of doing the work of God's reign in the world.

This is a way of being that increasingly strips us of our religious hypocrisy. Our discerning the truth and our laying down our lives work reciprocally. As we lay down our lives to God, in trusting God, we begin to see more clearly what has *not* been from God. With that discernment, we find we must continue to lay it all down. With every laying down of our lives, the false self dies and we are being empowered to take up the new life, our true selves. In this age of hypocrisy, the way forward is through laying it all down, not holding back from God what belongs to God: our very selves which come from God.

The laying down of our lives and taking up the new life, the dying and the rising, are one reality. They cannot be separated. While Jesus' death is central to the Christ-reality, Robin Meyers points out that the cross, "this icon of suffering and death, so central to Western Christianity, is absent from the art of the church for a thousand years." The art of the first centuries depicted restoration: "These images depict life, abundance, peace, and heaven coming down to earth—but no crucifixes."[43] It was in the European Middle Ages that a fixation on the cross at the expense of the resurrection developed along with what has been called the "satisfaction" and "penal substitution" explanations for Jesus' death. A rational explanation for the necessity of Jesus' death evolved along these lines: God is a God of righteousness and judgment who is offended by humanity's sin and demands a punishment for atonement. Jesus is the spotless "lamb of God" who steps into our place and takes the rap for us, fullfilling the demands of a righteous judge. It is not an attractive image of God, and it causes a split between the actions of God and God's self-revelation in Jesus. Growing up with this conception, I felt this division between Father and Son, and, as a child, I would confess my sins to Jesus rather than to God the Father. The "blood of Jesus" would cover my unrighteousness and avert the anger of the Father. This way of thinking about Jesus' death has held sway, in many churches, for centuries and continues in many churches today. It is not present in the New Testament, but if you have been taught this rationale for Jesus' death,

---

43. Meyers, *Underground Church*, 99.

you may think that you find it there and quote Scripture passages to prove it. In this way of thinking, there is an additional split between Jesus' death and resurrection. It is as if his death were *the* thing that makes us right with God and additional rationales, therefore, have to be given for the resurrection. In the early centuries of the church, as with the New Testament, this theological construct was not present; rather the emphasis was on the victory of the resurrection that liberates us from sin, death and the devil into new life. The emphasis was on what *God* has done through Christ. It is one action in which, through Christ, our Father/Mother goes out after prodigal sons and daughters to bring them home. The way home is through dying and rising, repenting and trusting. Jesus' death and resurrection are one reality, as it is for us through him.

FOLLOWING THE RISEN ONE

In the book of Acts, we are told that on the day Jesus' followers experienced an outpouring of the Spirit of God, Peter addressed the crowd that had gathered with these words:

> Jesus of Nazareth, a man attested to you by God with deeds of power, wonders, and signs that God did through him among you, as you yourselves know—this man, handed over to you according to the definite plan and foreknowledge of God, you crucified and killed by the hands of those outside the law. But God raised him up, having freed him from death, because it was impossible for him to be held in its power.[44]

Paul, whose writings are the earliest in the New Testament, writes to the church in Corinth, in about 53–54 CE, (about twenty years after his conversion):

> For I handed on to you as of first importance what I in turn had received: that Christ died for our sins in accordance with the scriptures, and that he was buried, and that he was raised on the third day in accordance with the scriptures, and that he appeared to Cephas, then to the twelve. Then he appeared to more than five hundred brothers and sisters at one time, most of whom are still alive, though some have died. Then he appeared to James, then to all the apostles. Last of all, as to one untimely born, he appeared also to me.[45]

---

44. Acts 2:22–24.
45. 1 Cor 15:3–8.

Paul writes of the appearances of the risen Jesus to the twelve, to over five hundred brothers and sisters, and then, last of all, to himself—making himself an eyewitness. It is these appearances, and the nature of their experience with the risen Jesus, that turned these followers of Jesus from despondency and despair into a movement that was "turning the world upside down."

What these first followers experienced in Jesus' resurrection was victory over death—over spiritual death. "For as all die in Adam, so all will be made alive in Christ."[46] Adam represents humanity in the condition of sin and spiritual death. Through Messiah Jesus' resurrection, all are made alive—alive to the Source of Life. Death has lost its sting. In Christ, that which is perishable is taken up into imperishability.[47] As Jesus was raised from the dead, so will all be raised in him. Believing this enables Paul to fight the good fight—otherwise "why are we putting ourselves in danger every hour? I die every day! . . . If with merely human hopes I fought with wild animals at Ephesus, what would I have gained by it?"[48] Paul is able to face death, to put himself in all manner of danger, because he believes that, like Christ and in Christ, he will be raised from the dead, in the age to come.

The reality of resurrection, however, is not for a future age alone, or for the way such a belief emboldens our actions now. Resurrection means new life now. It means victory over spiritual death. Jesus' death and resurrection is of one piece. It concerns dying to the power of the idolatrous self and becoming alive to our true selves and callings that come from God. We are freed from bondage to sin and made alive to God and God's purposes for us. Alive to God, we are empowered by God's Spirit. We gain both discernment to recognize what God is calling forth from us and the power to do it.

The book of Acts proclaims the continuation of Jesus' work—the work of God's reign. People are healed, delivered from the power of evil, and hear the good news of God's reign that comes through Jesus. From Acts and the letters of Paul, we enter communities and a movement empowered by the Spirit of God. These communities of faith are raised to a new life in the Spirit. The Spirit which raised Jesus from the dead raises men and women from being dead toward God to being alive to God. They become people who are led by the Spirit, rather than by their idolatrous selves—that which Paul calls the "flesh."[49]

---

46. 1 Cor 15:22.
47. 1 Cor 15:53–54.
48. 1 Cor 15:30–32.
49. Rom 8:1–12.

The resurrected life, here and now, is a life open to the Spirit's leading and empowering. Therefore, Paul writes of these early Christians' experience with gifts and ministries of the Spirit. As they are alive to God, it is not surprising that God acts within their communities in expressions of timely messages (prophetic utterances), words of wisdom, inspired teaching, acts of mercy and healings. It is also not surprising to see that these Christians experience themselves as sent out to others as witnesses to God's action.

Neither is it astonishing that their witness engendered opposition from those in authority and from the societies in which they lived. These participants in God's reign could no longer cooperate with, or engage in, the practices that had previously constituted their lives. They could not participate in the temple activities related to the various gods, practices that their contemporaries viewed as necessary for the social order. They could not bow down to the Roman emperor or support the enterprises of the empire as empire. They could work for the uplift of society, but as people experiencing God's reign.

Furthermore, in their witness to God's reign and to Jesus as Lord, they called others to turn from the worship of idols and turn to the true and living God. They called others away from emperor (and empire) worship. They called people to turn from the central aspects of Roman society to serve God with their whole selves. They radically disrupted the status quo. No wonder they experienced persecution: The new life conflicts with the old life!

In all these things, they, like Jesus, exhibit an authority that comes from a different place than that of this world. They talk and act like people who were sent from God, empowered by God and given authority for their actions from God. They simply operated from a different place. They had come to know the source of their lives and their callings in God.

Following the Risen One puts them, and puts us, on a journey of liberation and victory. We become "more than conquerors through him who loved us."[50] As we die to our idolatries, addictions, and obsessions, we rise up as children of God. We are on a journey of deliverance. We are coming to know the freedom of the children of God, the freedom of being led by the Spirit rather than driven by every sort of disoriented desire, attitude, or misplaced value. The resurrected life is life empowered by the Spirit, outward to others, to be witnesses. The Risen Jesus gathers us together and then leads us out into the world to be witnesses in word and action.

---

50. Rom 8:37.

8

Witness in An Age of Hypocrisy

In the act of following Jesus, our hypocrisy increasingly is stripped away and we become witnesses. Our false constructions of Christ are dismantled. Much of what we have called Christianity is overturned. As we experience God's judgment of our own hypocrisy ("For the time has come for judgment to begin with the household of God."[1]), we begin to discern God's ways and become witnesses, first to the household of God and then to the world.

Within the community of Jesus' followers, as we meditate on his teaching, grow in faithful obedience, and experience God's judgment, liberation, and guidance, we gain a sense of mission and singleness of purpose. We realize we are being sent into the world. In this way we are being prepared to witness before the world. Our first witness, however, is within the household of God.

We must be witnesses to others who call themselves Christians. Leaders in Christian communities, especially, are called to speak to other leaders and address today's hypocrisy and false Christianity. Jesus was not "nice" to those who led others astray. For the sake of those being led astray, as well as those doing the leading astray, Jesus spoke truth and called out hypocrisy. Church leaders today, as in every age, are tempted by power and elevated positions. They often do what they do for the sake of appearances, hide their false allegiances behind a facade of religiosity, deceiving themselves and others.[2] This tendency must be addressed within the Christian community and by church leaders.

---

1. 1 Pet 4:17.
2. "Beware of the scribes, who like to walk around in long robes, and to be greeted

The kind of evangelicalism and "Christian nationalism" that have been able to support Donald Trump, or prosperity religion, or legalistic fundamentalism are often what growing numbers of people distant from Christianity view as the religion of Christians. This Christianity is largely what gets broadcast by the media. Mainline historic denominations often receive little attention in the news, because many of their congregations are entrenched in cultural allegiances, middle-class values, moralism, and internal agendas. Their congregational life and mission, while lifting up aspects of God's reign, are often largely a project of human energy and effort. This often achieves burnout and does little to benefit the world.

Nevertheless, across denominations, there is a growing ecumenicity rooted in a shared history of grappling with Scripture text, foundational creeds, and theology, and an increasing openness to the world, movements away from defensive postures, and toward commitment to social justice. Still, much congregational witness remains timid. What is needed is a spiritual transformation and seriousness about following Jesus that issues forth in "dangerous preaching" and confrontation with Christian hypocrisy.[3] Where we encounter spiritual revival, and a prominent place given to prayer and the blossoming of ecumenical gatherings that are open to the Spirit, we see a fresh witness to God's reign. In faith communities, where following Jesus in the power of the Spirit is tangibly being lived out, true witness in word and action is manifest, often far from the limelight: storefront churches ministering to the streets, contemplative comunities exercising "sacred activism,"[4] ecumenical gatherings centered in word and Spirit, and historic mainline congregations reclaiming their mission as followers of Jesus. These and others are signs that contradict and expose the false Christianity that pervades our society.

Frederick Douglass, a former slave and a prophet, lectured extensively throughout the northern United States and Europe. He made a significant part of his speeches an exhortation, not only against the false Christianity of slavery-supporting churches in the South, but against northern churches that refused to cut ties with these slavery-supporting churches. Addressing the issue of humans held in bondage and brutalized, Douglass called out, with great clarity, the false Christianity that supported slavery. Something like this must be done today. A Christianity that supports the demeaning,

---

with respect in the marketplaces, and to have the best seats in the synagogues and places of honor at banquets! They devour widows' houses and for the sake of appearance say long prayers. They will receive the greater condemnation" (Mark 12:38–40).

3. See Thomas, *How to Preach A Dangerous Sermon*.

4. See McEntee and Bucko, *New Monasticism,* for their description of "sacred activism."

and even terrorizing, of immigrants, that supports the military as the solution to the issue of security, that supports a white nationalism, or does little to respond to the inequality and oppression rooted in racism, must be identified as a false Christianity. This form of Christianity no longer follows Jesus, the head of the church. Therefore the truth of God's reign and God's kind of governance must be regained and broadcast.

We realize that Jesus leads his followers out of the ways of the world, so that they increasingly operate in a manner counter to the "norms" of the world. Thus, they become witnesses to God's reign, over against the kingdoms of the world. As Jesus says:

> My kingdom is not from this world. If my kingdom were from this world, my followers would be fighting to keep me from being handed over to the Jews. But as it is, my kingdom is not from here.[5]

If we continue to follow Jesus, the world will take notice of our "peculiar" ways as they did with first-century Christians and in times of Christian renewal. For this witness to go beyond the witness of disparate individuals, churches must become communities of followers, moving out of long-adopted cultural patterns and into a life aligned with God's reign. Jesus, the head of the church, will lead us out of ways of being church that we have become comfortable with but have little or nothing to do with God's purpose for us—especially the ethnonationalism that has sidetracked the church for centuries.

We see signs of this nationalism in the way churches have adapted themselves to national celebrations, incorporating a nation's holidays into their worship life without recognizing the problematic nature of these activities. In subtle and not so subtle ways, the priorities and values of the nation have become entwined with a form of Christianity; the witness to God's reign has been diluted and even disappears.

Nationalism and racism combine to undermine our witness. The celebration of Independence Day is not the same as a Christian's celebration of the liberty found in Christ (which is the freedom of loving God and others), but they tend to get blended—and the meaning of Christ is lost when they are combined. The independence that gets celebrated in this national holiday is the independence of colonies from the tyranny of a king and colonizing nation. The independence that our nation celebrates is a rather narrow one; in its historical context, it is the independence of white people, as a white nation, and ignores the continued enslavement of people of African

---

5. John 18:36.

descent. Churches that celebrate "Independence Day" generally are oblivious to the celebration of "Juneteenth" in African American communities. Juneteenth is a holiday lifting up the independence of enslaved Africans on the date that the announcement of the abolition of slavery reached Texas, June Nineteenth, 1865. Furthermore, the Fourth of July holiday overlooks the history of the usurpment of land from and genocide done to indigenous peoples of the Americas. God's reign, however, does not pass over these other histories, or the sin and evil in our nation's formation. The Spirit of God reveals the truth of our human and communal condition before God. The Spirit leads us from perpetration of an American founding myth to repentance and a centering in God, in whom we receive the healing of our divisions (which is a foretaste of the "healing of the nations"[6]).

Memorial Day and Veterans Day add their own distortions to Christian worship and our centering in God. I preached in a congregation on Veterans Day; worship began with a color guard that brought into the worship space the symbolic protection and reverence for the nation's flag. This was a new experience for me and a jarring one. I suspect there are many other congregations that do something similar. This symbolic act does nothing for preparing a congregation for the worship of the one, true God. Instead, into the gathering, it brings symbols that idolize a nation and undermine the inclusiveness of God's people.

These national holidays divide us in relation to the experiences of the various peoples who make up the United States. They also divide us from other nations. As such, they go against the Christian's confession that the church is one, holy, and catholic (universal). It is global; it knows no boundaries. It is one with people of faith of every time and place, our oneness being in God.

Nations will have their days of remembrance and celebration. Christians can decide how to engage in them, as we enter into the various activities of our fellow citizens. But our gatherings around the word, in openness to the Spirit, are for the purpose of worship and renewal, and for our being sent back into the world to do God's will, which includes ministry to those who have been traumatized by war—soldier and civilian alike. When we follow Jesus, our relationship to our nation's values and the ways of our society changes. We will no longer expect pastors to preach a message that intermingles nationalist and militarist views with a form of Christianity, but instead will expect a word that calls us to repent from such views. As we increasingly follow Jesus into God's reign, we move out into the world,

---

6. Rev 22:2.

above all, as citizens of the kingdom of God. Our witness is to God's reign, liberation, and mercy and it is directed to all people.

Prior to Adolph Hitler becoming chancellor in 1933, there was a German Christian movment that was ethnonationalist, anti-Semitic and supportive of the Nazi Party. Hitler played to the sentiments of this movement in a fashion similar to the way politicians today hook into a Christian nationalism, with electoral success. In a 1932 letter to his grandmother, Dietrich Bonhoeffer wrote of the developing struggle:

> It is becoming increasingly clear to me that what we are going to get is a big, völkisch [ethnic] national church that in its essence can no longer be reconciled with Christianity, and that we must make up our minds to take entirely new paths and follow where they lead. The issue is really Germanism or Christianity, and the sooner the conflict comes out in the open, the better. The greatest danger of all would be in trying to conceal this.[7]

The issue for Bonhoeffer and the Confessing Church (which stood against the heresy of the "German Church") was that Jesus Christ is Lord and must be followed in obedient faith in the midst of the idolatry of the people and the state. And this "Christian" idolatry of nation and race must not remain concealed. It must be exposed by a true following of Jesus.

In the strain of Christian ethnonationalism of our time, which crosses denominations, a Christian moralism (commandments and laws) is a cover for an underlying idolatry of nation and race and the idea of a "Christian" nation with a normative culture that is implicitly white. In Bonhoeffer's words, "the greatest danger of all would be in trying to conceal this." What would be concealed is a church of laws rather than of grace and capable of great injustice and hurt. Therefore, what must be exposed is a moralistic Christianity bereft of the Spirit. The followers of Jesus are to be witnesses that bring to light what has been hidden so that others are not led astray and those in bondage are freed. We are to be light within the household of God and then to the world. When our witness to the world comes from following Jesus, it brings light to the world and, at the same time, exposes the prevalent false Christianity of our age.

CALLED TO BE LIGHT

> You are the light of the world. A city built on a hill cannot be hid. No one after lighting a lamp puts it under the bushel basket,

---

7. Bonhoeffer, *Theological Education*, 11.

but on the lampstand, and it gives light to all in the house. In the same way, let your light shine before others, so that they may see your good works and give glory to your Father in heaven.[8]

In the message of the book of Revelation, when God's reign has come in its fullness, there is no need for light. The city of God "has no need of sun or moon to shine on it, for the glory of God is its light, and its lamp is the Lamb. The nations will walk by its light, and the kings of the earth will bring their glory into it."[9] "And there will be no more night; they need no light of lamp or sun, for the Lord God will be their light, and they will reign forever and ever."[10] The light of the glory of God is all that is needed. We await that "age to come." It is only because of the darkness of our present age that there is need for light. And so Jesus says to his community of followers, "You are the light of the world." Jesus' followers are to shine in the darkness. They are to be witnesses to the one who is the Light through whom all become light.[11]

Because of the present darkness, God calls forth a people who will be light. God gathers us from the darkness, into the light, and makes us light. "For once you were darkness, but now in the Lord you are light. Live as children of light."[12] We must be clear about this: We cannot remain in the darkness and be light. Not everyone who calls themselves Christian lives by the name to which they have attached themselves. Not everyone with a theology or the ability to engage in God-talk has come into the light. Jesus says to his *followers*, "You are the light of the world." It is in the following, in the obedience of faith, that we become a light in the darkness.

So, what is it like to be light in the darkness? What is it like for communities of faith to be light? Jesus tells his followers that, as light, they shine;

---

8. Matt 5:13–16.

9. Rev 21:23–24.

10. Rev 22:5.

11. As the Gospel of John puts it, "Jesus spoke to them, saying, 'I am the light of the world. Whoever follows me will never walk in darkness but will have the light of life'" (John 8:12). As people of the light, Jesus' followers are to be light. Each of the Gospels lifts up the notion of light, but it is John's Gospel that works with the themes of light and darkness throughout. Starting with the first chapter, Jesus' life, as the Word of God in the flesh, is "the light of all people" (John 1:4). He is the light that "shines in the darkness" and that the darkness does not overcome (John 1:5). He is the light that enlightens everyone (John 1:9). Judgment is seen in the rejection of the light that has come into the world because people preferred darkness (John 3:19–20). People stumble "because the light is not in them" and they do not know where they are going (John 11:9, 12:35). John connects light and faith: "While you have the light, believe in the light, so that you may become children of light" (John 12:36). Jesus' purpose for coming into the world is "that everyone who believes in me should not remain in the darkness" (John 12:46).

12. Eph 5:8.

they are not hidden. Like lamps, they are light "for all in the house." As witnesses to what God desires for humanity they are light. Their actions, when their source is in God, are light. This is why we know them by their fruits. Their fruits, which include what comes out of their mouths, express their source.

Individuals may put themselves forward as children of light; their words and actions either confirm or betray them. On the one hand, there are those who make much religious noise, but that which comes forth from them is neither light nor love. On the other, there are those who make little noise about being children of the light, but what they say and do shows that they are light. This is true not only of individuals but of faith communities as well. In this age of hypocrisy, it is the light that exposes lies and false ways, exposing the playacting for what it is. The light both exposes the works of darkness and reveals the ways of God. Followers of Jesus are witnesses. Therefore, children of light, let your light so shine before others that they may encounter God's will for humanity!

EMPOWERED FOR WITNESS

Here are the words of the risen Jesus in the Gospel of Luke: "You are witnesses of these things. And see, I am sending upon you what my Father promised; so stay here in the city until you have been clothed with power from on high."

The followers of Jesus, who are being sent as witnesses in an age of hypocrisy, are "clothed with power from on high." There is, of course, a relationship between the staying (they are told to stay where they were in the city) and the being clothed with power. There is a connection between the waiting on God and the receiving of help and power. In order to be witnesses to the Christ reality and to what God wills for us in the present, we must wait for the Spirit, be led by the Spirit, and receive both discernment for next steps and words to speak. ("When they bring you to trial and hand you over, do not worry beforehand about what you are to say; but say whatever is given you at that time, for it is not you who speak, but the Holy Spirit."[13])

When the clear word of truth goes forth, with an outpouring of the Spirit, we can expect a revival of the church and its true mission of compassion and love. The Jesus movement, in its beginnings, was a movement of truth in the power of the Spirit, starting with Jesus, upon whom the Spirit was poured. It continued with his followers, upon whom the Spirit also was poured. These followers were released into a mission, empowered for

13. Mark 13:11.

ministry and to proclaim the good news of God's reign, which—through Jesus—was breaking in upon the world. Ministry, empowered and inspired by the Spirit, is seen in works of compassion, healing, encouragement, liberation, and social justice. In churches where doing justice is emphasized, the renewing work of the Spirit results in new energy for showing mercy and confronting injustice—including injustice within the church. However, if our theological constructs provide little place for social justice, we often constrict the work of the Spirit and diminish the larger social dimension of ministry. This situation generally remains until our constructs are transformed.

The commitment to follow Jesus in obedience to his teaching and to his vision of God's reign forces us to ask for the Spirit's help. We cannot do this work without the Helper any more than the first followers could. There are two accounts of the giving of the Spirit, one in Acts and the other in the Gospel of John. In John, the disciples are behind locked doors for fear of the Judean authorities. Suddenly, the risen Jesus appears to them with the signs of his suffering and death still on his body. To these followers who have hidden themselves away from the world to which they were sent to be witnesses, Jesus speaks words of sending, "Peace be with you. As the Father has sent me, so I send you." But not only words of sending does he give them. He breathes on them and says, "Receive the Holy Spirit."[14] Their release from fear to bold witness only happens when they are empowered by the Spirit of God.

In Luke-Acts,[15] the risen Jesus reminds his disciples that "repentance and forgiveness of sins is to be proclaimed in his name to all nations, beginning from Jerusalem." They are to be witnesses. Therefore, Jesus tells them to wait to be "clothed with power from on high."[16] They did as Jesus instructed and, on the Day of Pentecost, the Spirit was poured out on them and they began to proclaim the message of God's Anointed, the message of God's reign, with boldness.[17] The transformation from scared followers to bold witnesses was the work of the Spirit. The followers' job was simply to wait and be open to the Spirit.

Jesus and his message cannot be separated from the Spirit that empowers both. If we, as proclaimers, and our message are separated from the Spirit, we lose our way and our witness. When we lose our way and become

---

14. John 20:19–23.

15. At the end of the Gospel of Luke and at the beginning of Acts, the author of these two books writes of the promise and sending of the Spirit.

16. Luke 24:49.

17. Acts 1–2.

distant from the Spirit and source of our lives, we end up attempting to make Jesus' words conform to our false selves. In our congregations, we turn inward, to our own self-crafted fellowships. Our Christian wordage remains, but hides what is false. Of course, this is always a tendency and struggle for individuals and congregations. That is why, when we get truthful, we acknowledge that we need revival.

THE POWER OF LIGHT

Jesus, the light of the world, exposed the works of darkness. He cut through the false facades. He did not let the play-acting of religious leaders remain a cover for evil. He called out the "scribes and the Pharisees" who "sit on Moses' seat." While they were learned men from whom people could receive teaching, Jesus warned people to "not do as they do, for they do not practice what they teach." Jesus made clear that these hypocrites laid heavy burdens on others. They did not enter God's kingdom and prevented others from doing so. They loved places of honor. They liked to be seen with those in positions of authority—much like today, when Christian leaders cozy up to power as a way to obtain a privileged position for themselves and their people. Jesus called out religious leaders who were "blind guides." He called them out for their legalistic focus on minor issues, while neglecting the weightier matters of "justice and mercy and faith." They made much of outward behavior, while, on the inside, they were "full of greed and self-indulgence."[10]

Jesus exposed arrogance and deception. Notice the contrast to the way the Scribes and Pharisees called people out for their behavior. Consider the story of the woman caught in adultery. They accused her, took her out into the street, and prepared to stone her to death. Jesus, addressing them, reminded them of their sin ("Let anyone among you who is without sin be the first to throw a stone at her."[19]). When he addressed the woman, he did not condemn her or further expose her, but spoke words of mercy and forgiveness and called her to turn from her past and walk in a new way.[20]

Notice, also, that for which the religious leaders accused Jesus: healing on the Sabbath,[21] letting a man know that his sins were forgiven,[22] eating

---

18. Matt 23:1–36.
19. John 8:7.
20. John 8:10–11.
21. Luke 14:1–6; John 5:1–8, 7:23.
22. Mark 2:1–2; Luke 5:17–26.

with tax collectors (traitors) and other sinners,[23] letting a woman who was a "sinner" touch him,[24] and ignoring legalistic rules (allowing his followers to pluck heads of grain on the Sabbath).[25] Jesus in turn called them to the weightier matters of God's reign: justice, mercy, and faith.[26] Those weightier matters critique what we make an issue of today.

They raise questions for religious leaders who worry people over so-called "traditional values," which often on closer observation look more like older cultural traditions (gender roles, for example) than Christian ones. These weightier matters expose the attitudes that get expressed toward other religions ("Islam is a hateful religion," proclaims a religious leader). They bring to light the dominant (and often skewed) focus on sexual and gender mores (anxiety over transgender persons in public bathrooms, for example) that blind us to the injustices present in these attitudes while ignoring other major injustices of our time. These weightier matters of Jesus also critique the orientation of "prosperity churches" to "sowing seeds" in order to elicit prosperity from God. What does such a "gospel" have to do with trust in God and God's will in doing justice, loving mercy, and walking humbly with God? Also, many historic mainline congregations, who mouth the language of justice and mercy, are exposed for failing to walk by faith into the reality.

While there is a place for exposing hypocrisy, especially of leaders, it is important for us to notice that not all calling out others is the same. It is one thing to ridicule vulnerable people for their brokenness; it is another to call out the lack of mercy toward broken people and name the injustices in our society. It is particularly easy to call out others' sins when we do not perceive those sins as being our own. It is, then, easy to act as though those are *the* sins that corrupt our society, all the while being blind to our self-righteousness that cuts us off from the true needs of others. What we notice about Jesus is that he does not call out the vulnerable and publicly shame them, or add to the burdens they are already carrying. He calls out those in positions of authority who unjustly exercise power over the lives of others. To those who are broken, needy, and sinning, he reaches out in mercy with healing and liberation. To all, he proclaims God's reign and calls people to turn to God with their whole selves.

When people come to Jesus with their troubles, he ministers compassionately. At times, he *exposes* that which is getting in the way of their relationship with God and others. A man asks Jesus to intervene for him

23. Mark 2:16.
24. Luke 7:37–39.
25. Matt 12:1–7; Mark 2:23–28; Luke 6:1–5.
26. Matt 23:23.

with his brother over the issue of their inheritance; Jesus speaks to the man's root problem, the thing he does not see: his greed. Then Jesus speaks to the crowd about this common problem.[27] To a man paralyzed, Jesus brings to light the hidden spiritual problem of guilt by declaring God's forgiveness to the man. To a Pharisee, in whose house he is dining, Jesus gently but firmly exposes the self-righteousness that gets in the way of his host's loving, being hospitable, and seeing others' needs.[28] In the Gospel of John, the stories of Jesus' personal encounters with Nicodemus and the Samaritan woman at the well provide examples of Jesus bringing to light what is hidden and revealing the underlying spiritual reality.[29]

In personal encounters, Jesus is penetrating in exposing what must be brought to light. However, he does this work with compassion, like a physician who must do surgery in order to allow healing. Jesus speaks the truth—the hard truth—in love. We see him take his disciples aside to talk about what it means to be great in God's kingdom (serving others). He is not out to shame them. And when Jesus calls out people publicly, he does so to unmask the deceit and falsehoods that often hide under the cover of religion and deceive others. He warns people not to be deceived by the lies of those in authority, but to know them by their actions.

Followers of Jesus are to operate in the same way today. As the Spirit gives us discernment, we must address what hurts and demeans others, robbing them of their true humanity. We must proclaim and minister God's liberating work. In relation to those who lead people astray, we cannot stand aside and say nothing. We must, as the Spirit leads, expose the works of darkness and call out the hypocrisy. I am a member of a church where the pastor periodically addresses people who have been hurt by churches they have attended and then addresses church people who hurt others through their self-righteousness. Part of the process of healing for those hurt is in the acknowledgment and exposure of the oppressive ways of others toward them. They are being affirmed in their experience.

It is clear that the gathering of Jesus' followers is not centered on maintaining church doctrine or keeping traditions; the essential focus is to listen and then witness to what we have heard, in the present moment, addressing the hurts of individuals as well as the issues and conditions of our time. As Jesus was led by the Spirit to speak to individuals, to groups of people, and to those in authority, so must followers of Jesus do today.

---

27. Luke 12:13–15.
28. Luke 7:36–50.
29. John 3:1–21, 4:1–30.

We do not do this by spending the majority of our time attending to organizational issues, music ministry, appealing worship, how to be a "friendly" church, property, or finances. We expect that with a group of Jesus' followers, for whom the word and Spirit are central and worship flows forth in gifts for ministry, the organization is being supported and the word and mission of God's reign is going forth into the world. The Spirit leads us out from the waiting, praying, and worship into the streets, into the highways and byways, to persuade others to come into God's reign and do the works of light. A word goes forth from the gathering into the world, a word that addresses the conditions of individuals and society. Actions of justice and mercy take form in our neighborhoods and nation.

As people who are sent, we are light in the world. We witness to what comes from the source of our lives, as we discover it. As we follow Jesus and as Christ is formed in us, we increasingly become a sign to the world of what God is saying and doing. We act prophetically, as the Spirit directs us, speaking a word that is timely and addresses present injustices. We are active in doing justice, loving mercy, and living faithfully.

We become increasingly open to our world, to what is happening around us. We learn to pay attention, gain knowledge, and understanding. We are not adverse to the various ways that knowledge comes and grows in us. All truth is God's truth.

Truth continues to work its way into us in order that it may be expressed through us. With the help of the Spirit of truth, we increasingly gain self-awareness and recognize attitudes, disoriented desires, fears, and prejudices from which we must turn away daily, in order to remain open and receptive. We gain freedom. Where the Spirit is, there is freedom. In that freedom, we are given eyes to see; a veil is being removed from our spiritual eyes. We hear more clearly God's call to do justice. We more clearly understand the inequities of our world, why there is poverty, how capitalism and the other "isms"—militarism, nationalism, racism, materialism, and so on—generate the breakdown of society. In all these things, we are witnesses to God's call and action.

We are becoming open. We see what the pollution of our planet by human beings is doing and what catastrophes are being handed on to future generations. We are not opposed to knowledge, to scientific knowledge, that helps us to see what is happening to our planet—and why. Rising oceans, polluted air and water, endangered plants and animals, and the ongoing change of climate with its catastrophic consequences become impossible to ignore. We know we are called to be stewards of the earth's resources. As followers of Jesus, we, who expect that all things will be brought together in God, are freed to view our global community for the long term. We do not live for short-term gains, but for long-term vision. We are being freed to care about the mass migrations and massive disruptions that the changing climate will produce, if not addressed. We know we are called to do justice—that is, to right what is wrong—and join with others in this task. We are to show mercy for those who come after us. David Wallace-Wells, in his book, *The Uninhabitable Earth: Life after Warming*, believes that it may take panic finally to shake the world out of its lethargy so that action is taken to avert the worst of the worst effects of global warming.[30] For serious followers of Jesus, we would expect love to take action long before fear. But love must be engaged politically to address this immense global issue, and we must join with others who have eyes to see and hearts to act.

We must address racism and white supremacy, a responsibility that love places acutely on those of us who are white and who have come to confess our racism. White follower of Jesus, are you not finding that you no longer have to defend yourself in regards to racism? Has the Spirit of truth not convinced you of your broken condition? We who are white and *following* Jesus and being led by the Spirit are being freed to recognize what is going on inside us, exposing attitudes and defenses, and enabling us to recognize our participation in the racism that is part of the fabric of our society. We are being freed to listen to, and truly hear, what others affected by our racism share with us about its effects. We are being made open, to gain knowledge and to recognize the existence of structural, systemic racism. We, who are white, as we become open, realize that our experience with the police, with corporations, with political power, is not the same as that of people of color. Our "whiteness" has historically—and still does—privilege us. We have not been able to see this clearly, in the way, for example, people of African descent recognize it. But they can help us. We can grow in understanding by listening. How else do we receive what others are experiencing, except by listening? And how can we love others without receiving? (If, among the books we read, there are no writings by African Americans, then we are likely not listening.) As we receive what the Spirit is revealing to us through others, we become witnesses, not only in speech, but in actions to dismantle the structures built by racism: an unjust criminal justice system, mistreatment of immigrants, economic, educational, and health care inequalities, and other systemic and institutionalized practices produced by white supremacy. (By "white supremacy," I am referring to a history of white law-making, mores, and practices that established and maintained slavery, Jim Crow, the mass incarceration of people of color, and present day

---

30. Wallace-Wells, *The Uninhabitable Earth*. "Panic" is a word the author uses throughout the book.

inequities.) Our understanding and witness flows from our listening and receiving. We need what God gives to us through others.

Followers of Jesus are learning to recognize their poverty. There is no way to follow Jesus, who became poor for us, and not increasingly realize our poverty and need. We are helpless without the help of God. It is from a place of poverty—spiritual poverty—that we become open to God and available to other needy people. It is impossible to follow Jesus and not be led to other needy people: materially needy, spiritually needy, hurting, broken, grieving. In Christ, the barriers of classism and racism increasingly are broken down. Jesus went to the poor, and by following Jesus, we cannot do otherwise. We are all in need of God and one another. What is there that can come between us and another human being, in Christ? We, who have been maturing in following Jesus, know that someone who is materially very wealthy can have a greater poverty than those materially poor, for their wealth makes it hard for them to enter the reign of God.[31] Their wealth separates them from much of the rest of humanity in such a way that they are impoverished of human reality. But since we recognize their poverty—whether they do or not—we realize that they are not so distant from us. And yet the idolatry of riches can make the rich distant from God and others. On the other hand, those that know they are poor and needy are often ready for the good news of God's reign. They know they need God. That God is near, loves them, and makes a way for them is good news.

GAINING CLARITY AND DIRECTION

As we persist in following Jesus, moving out to a broken world, we continue to gain greater clarity about ourselves, the false and the true. We go deeper into what is going on inside us, letting the Spirit help us to die to what is not from God and to lead us into God's ways. We are on a journey. We do not need to worry about our brokenness and need, as it is merely a condition of which we are becoming increasingly aware. We simply know that discerning our brokenness is an aspect of the help that the Spirit of truth brings to us. It is the increasing light in the darkness. We can be grateful for what it exposes, because what we see is what the light of God reveals. We see the disorder because we increasingly see order. As we journey into God's call into our true selves we grow in discerning what is false. At times, we may feel overwhelmed by what is being revealed but our helplessness increases our desire for what God is doing in us. We desire the dying and the rising

---

31. Matt 19:23–24.

and are drawn more deeply into the Christ reality. We look forward with hope to what God still has in store for the growth of our true selves.

In this journey, the obedience of faith is critical. Following means we take the steps given to us. There are aspects of our condition that would prevent us from taking steps. We can become comfortable with our attitudes, ideologies, politics, and theologies. Especially our theologies. We often look for security in what we have been taught to believe, rather than trusting in the God to which beliefs point. Experience and faith come first; then, reflection, beliefs, and theology. We can receive the reflections of another that help us toward the experience, but, until we have our own experience, we cannot truly understand and reflect the reality. Our reflections also are continually broken up by new experiences of what God is doing. As we experience more, earlier truth is seen as partial. However, in order to experience the "more" that God has for us, we must be open and receptive, not holding onto past understandings as though they were security blankets. We must not fear the truth, wherever or however it comes to us. Rather, fear not being open. Ask God to keep us open and seeking. By seeking, we find. Following Jesus means we continually leave the old behind. As Jesus tells us, "No one puts new wine into old wineskins . . . but one puts new wine into fresh wineskins."[32]

Taking seriously that we are on a journey and must take one step after another (and all must take their own steps as given to them) means that we cannot force others to be where we think they should be. Within the gathering of Jesus' followers there must be freedom for all to find their various ways. I learned, as a pastor, that it was important for me to listen and discern from what was shared by the one who came to me for guidance. They generally knew the next step they were being called to take, but were resisting because of some false dependency in their life. Often, my job was simply to help them clarify what they already knew. God works with each of us and there is a time for everything. This also means that we must not judge others from where we are on *our* journey. After all, we all have idols and addictions that tempt, ensnare, and sidetrack us, and, therefore, we are in no postion to be judges over others. We are to witness to the truth God gives us, but we then must leave the rest to the Spirit. For pastors, the proclaimed word within services of worship gives the opportunity to declare strong messages; some will be ready to hear and others will reject what they hear. We are not to refrain from speaking the hard truth. We must encourage followers of Jesus to keep seeking; that which they do not see now, they may see later. However, they must expect hard truth, because they are following Jesus, who spoke such truth.

---

32. Mark 2:22.

We expect that a growing, maturing community of Jesus' followers will increasingly be involved in the world in doing justice, loving mercy, and living faithfully. Such a community will be a sign that is opposed. There will be those who have wrapped themselves in a false religion of Christian rhetoric and nationalism; they will throw the accusation "atheists" at Jesus' faithful followers today, as was done to early Christians because they did not believe in the gods, among them the god of the Roman emperor (the nationalism of their day). Increasingly, congregations must see themselves as the concrete expression of Christ in the world, reaching out to the world in mercy and standing up against injustice.

Becoming expressions of Christ in the world happens as people expect radical change, both the kind that is immediate[33]—making the foundational decision to turn our lives over to God—and the progressively radical change that comes from daily following where Jesus leads, through the work of the Spirit. Proclamation and witness must provide a vision of God's reign breaking in upon our present moment. Response to the vision creates a community of faith where individual needs are addressed: needs for forgiveness, healing, and deliverance from various forms of bondage. Until we experience freedom from addictions and obsessions, we can hardly respond to the vision that sends us out into the world. Past hurts need healing, through the forgiving of others and the renewal of self-esteem. The Spirit activates gifts and various forms of serving for this purpose. The experience of God's reign within the gathered community prepares individuals for being sent into the world to be witnesses.

The community of Jesus' followers must maintain the connection between the personal and the communal. In Paul's words, we, who make up the body of Christ, are individually members of one body. The health of the individual is related to the health of the body, so that if one member hurts, the whole body hurts. Consider the body of Christ as it exists in the world. We who are followers of Jesus are engaged in the world and we are not unaffected by its evils. We hurt with the pain of the world and feel the disorder of the world; we also are afflicted and torn. We bring our wounds into the gathering of Jesus' followers and, with the gifts of the Spirit, we learn to minister to one another, so that each can go back into the world with good news and with hope. We must address afflictions both within and outside the gathering. Our serving one another lays a foundation for serving others in the world. As we follow Jesus and attend to one another's wounds, we become increasingly conscious of the effects of evil in the world. We are affected; along with the world, we are spiritually sickened. We are bruised

---

33. "Immediately they left their nets and followed him" (Mark 1:18).

and maimed, but within the gathered community we are also being healed. However, our process of recovery is clearly long-term, as we await the fullness of God's reign.

Increasingly, the Spirit enables us to discern and identify the various forms of evil in the world that tempt us personally: society's glorification of violence, its attraction to the sensational and titillating, its hero worship and celebrity fixation, its lust, pornography and greed, its materialist dismissal of the spiritual and its self-absorption. Christians, generally, recognize the evils of the world listed in the preceding sentence, but many, as far as their actions are concerned, minimize or operate oblivious to other crushing forms of evil. Racism, nationalism, and privileged social position blind Christians to the depth of impact on others of various societal sins. These take such forms of evil as the injustice of the mass incarceration of people of color and the poor (in prison, out of mind), police shootings, the treatment of migrants at our borders and within our borders, hate speech and organized hateful actions toward others that are deemed different, sexual harassment and abuse in the workplace, the stress of poverty, unequal access to education and health care, and the continual mobilization for war. For some, the effect of these evils are matters of life and death. For others, they are felt to be negligibly present in daily life. Paul says that we are individually members of one body, but often it seems there are two bodies: one has its personal experiences of evil in the "temptations of the flesh;" the other has, in addition to these forms of evil, the experience of social injustice and oppression with the resulting temptations to despair. For the body to be truly one and be able to speak with one voice to the world, members must genuinely listen to other members, enter into their afflictions and together share in the hope of the gospel.

Follow Jesus and he will lead us out of our enclaves. Jesus led his followers out to wilderness places where all manner of people gathered around him, hoping for relief. People who were anxious about food and clothing came to Jesus in the wilderness. Lepers who lived outside the community, the blind, the lame, and the sick came to him. People oppressed by those in positions of power and people bound by demonic evil came to him. And Jesus mentored his followers in ministry to these people. His followers learned to hear their cries and respond with compassion. The same situation exists for us today. Jesus sends his followers "into the streets and lanes" to "bring in the poor, the crippled, the blind, and the lame."[34] We are to bring them into the liberation and healing of God's reign. This is the holistic mission of the one body in Messiah Jesus.

---

34. Luke 14:21.

The message and action of God's reign are bound together. The proclamation engendered by the nearness of God's reign is "turn to God." Make up your mind now, trust your life to God in whom there is liberation and life. In fact, there are signs of the kingdom's nearness: "the blind receive their sight, the lame walk, the lepers are cleansed, the deaf hear, the dead are raised, and the poor have good news brought to them."[35] Where there is healing and hope, joy and uplift, and the freedom of the children of God, there God's reign is manifest. And we are witnesses to what God is doing.

JOINING WITH OTHERS

The followers of Jesus are not the only ones with compassion, committed to working for change. People of other faith communities have similar yearnings for justice and mercy as they experience the nearness of God, the source of their lives. It should not surprise Christians, who believe God is near, that others have experienced God's presence. If the Word became flesh and dwelt among us, God being joined to our humanity, then we can expect that others have come to be on a spiritual journey. Many years ago, as a seminarian, I read a book by a Norwegian Lutheran missionary to China, Karl Reichelt (1877–1952), who became a scholar of Buddhism and founded the Nordic Christian Buddhist Mission, a meeting place for Buddhist monks and Christians. The book that I read, entitled *The Transformed Abbott*, gave an account of the spiritual journey of a Buddhist monk who became a Christian.[36] As I recall, the first two-thirds of this book provides an account of this monk's spiritual journey before he became a Christian. His Buddhist journey, which included his discovery of Pure-Land Buddhism, had elements I recognized in my own journey and which I had associated with Christian experience. I recognized his experience of relinquishment to the source of life and his experience of grace. In the limited reading I have done of various sacred texts of Buddhism, Hinduism, and Islam, I have often recognized aspects of my own spiritual experience, although, at times, in alternate forms of expression. There is a spiritual wisdom and truth that transcends cultures. It is there for a humanity that is open.

It is not surprising that followers of Jesus increasingly have found common ground with their cousins, the followers of Prophet Muhammad and their parent, the people of the covenant, as well as those whose journeys have taken them through Eastern spirituality. As Jesus leads us out of our enclaves, we come to recognize our common bond with others who

---

35. Matt 11:4–5.
36. Reichelt, *The Transformed Abbott*.

are spiritually open. (We also recognize—similar to ours—the corruption of these other traditions by ethnonationalism.) And not only with those who see themselves as people of faith, but also with those who do not identify with any spiritual tradition, but welcome humanity—both their own and that of others. Those who open their hearts to others (who are "made in the image of God") cannot be far from God. Above all, we must join with others in the pursuit of social justice, so that we, along with others, do what God commands: "Let justice roll down like waters, and righteousness like an ever-flowing stream."[37]

I have been involved with faith-based community organizations for many years. These organizations have addressed such issues as equitable funding of education, affordable housing, transit disparities, urban food deserts, green jobs, economic injustice, and injustices in the criminal justice system. These organizations were led by clergy and people of faith. They were mainly Christian, although some included Jewish and Muslim leaders. All were welcome, but the leadership was made up of people of faith. Recently, however, I attended a social justice organization meeting that was not faith-based. It included clergy and people of faith, but it had a diversity of ethnic groups, urban and suburban, religious and non-religious (agnostic and atheist), all of which were represented in the leadership. What we had in common was a commitment to social justice. I appreciated the nature of this organization. Christians did not have a privileged place. We were one group among many others in the organization. We were engaged in a common mission of bringing about change in our society, oriented to justice. We shared from a place of faith—of a particular faith. Others shared from other places. We served the common good along with others. We were what Jesus called us to be, salt, light, and yeast; we effected decisions while not "lording it over others." We must be engaged in the world in order to be salt, light, and yeast; being engaged with others in a common mission means that we embrace the gifts and visions of others.

Early on in the program at this particular gathering various groups (perhaps a dozen) were given an opportunity to make some noise indicating their presence among us. By the level of noise, it was clear there was a sizable number of faith leaders. I was grateful for this witness that linked our faith to social justice, especially given that many, with little experience with Christians, have (through the media) associated Christians with reactionary impulses: anti-immigrant, anti-gay, anti-others, narrow, mean-spirited, and judgmental. The impression is often that Christians are looking out for themselves and pressing for a privileged place for Christianity in American

37. Amos 5:24.

society and law. I also recognized that the presence and witness of people of faith may encourage refugees who come from a distorted Christianity.

An African American pastor ended the meeting with a prayer. Before praying, he acknowledged that what he was about to do came from his faith tradition and that there were many others who did not share in this tradition or in any faith tradition. He encouraged others to reach out to God in the way *they* thought of God, or, if they did not believe in God, to simply share in the spirit of the work we were doing together. He did not speak from a place of special privilege, but from a place alongside others and as a servant to others. Certainly, this is where Jesus, who was the servant of all, has called us to be.[38] We have something to contribute when we take our places alongside others and share in the work for change directed toward justice and healing in our society. We, like others, strive for answers to the specific issues facing us. If we were to act like we were the ones with the answers, we would be no help. We need all who have a heart for justice and are willing to work with others. We add our witness, what we see, as we seek God's guidance. Being engaged in this manner also means that we have to accept the group decision. There may be times when we cannot accept a particular course of action, but this does not mean that we have a license to threaten to leave the organization or try to manipulate outcomes. We are servants in this work and there are generally other decisions and other actions to which we can give ourselves whole-heartedly.

Some Christians may raise the issue of Paul's admonition not to be "unequally yoked" (KJV), or "Do not be mismatched with unbelievers" (NRSV). The language gets stronger: "For what partnership is there between righteousness and lawlessness? Or what fellowship is there between light and darkness? What agreement does Christ have with Beliar? Or what does a believer share with an unbeliever?"[39] The issue is "fellowship," and the next sentence—"What agreement has the temple of God with idols?"—points to Paul's primary concern, which is Christians maintaining "fellowship" in temples to idols. There were many reasons some Christians continued their association with pagan temples. They joined others for meals, particularly those with whom they had business or with whom they shared a trade. These were places where the images of the human idolatry of self and society held sway over hearts and minds. Here, the mismatch is with the empire and the gods that support it. Paul's concern is with a partnership between those who

---

38. These reflections, at least in part, are taken from my blog post, "Privileged Or Servant," at neglectedmatters.com.

39. 2 Cor 6:14–15.

trust their lives to God and those who worship ego and nation—and the various idols that support them.

We have seen what happens with this kind of "mismatch." We have seen a form of Christianity taken up into the interests of nation, military, and political power. We have seen it become subservient to values far from those of Christ. We have seen its involvement in the same kinds of deceit and manipulation of others that worship at the altar of power produces. We have seen religious leaders become enamored with access to those in positions of power and become willing to go along with ways of operating that are far from the way in which Jesus calls us to walk. We have seen a form of Christianity that would lord it over others, rather than walk in the way of servanthood.

When we follow Jesus in doing justice and loving mercy, there is freedom to join others who also see injustice and oppression and want to work for change. We *must* join with others to serve and be "yeast," affecting the whole. This is our calling. We are not called by Jesus to disengage ourselves from humanity, but to welcome humanity, as God calls forth what is true and fitting to God's image. Jesus tells his followers, "Whoever is not against us is for us."[40] If someone is active in doing justice, loving mercy, and walking faithfully (what Jesus calls the "weightier matters"), we must encourage them, for this walk is a movement related to the source of their lives. On the other hand, if we cosign others' racism and nationalism, if we engage with others in fear, if we support others in trying to secure a privileged place, even when it is for "Christianity," we work in opposition to the Spirit and, in these ways, cease to follow where Jesus leads.

God calls us into the work of God's reign wherever that work is happening. We are to work for change by doing justice, loving mercy, and living faithfully. From that activity, we proclaim the good news that God is a God of justice and is merciful and faithful. Declaring the good news is clearly at the center of what the followers of Jesus are called to do. We are witnesses to God's mercy and forgiveness, as we have experienced it. We are witnesses to God's justice; it is merciful and restorative, not counting our sin against us, but aimed to deliver and heal us. And God has been faithful, when we have not. The God who is love does not give up on us.

Our journey forward is a journey of breaking free of our false selves and coming into our true selves in Christ. It is a journey of gaining openness to the truth, being set free and coming alive to God. We often feel the burden of our false self, our ego-centric thoughts and ways, our dishonesty and hypocrisy. As we follow Jesus, empowered by the Spirit, we are being remade, and the old is in the process of passing away. And yet the old false self

---

40. Mark 9:40–41.

still hangs on. We feel it in our loneliness and longing. We long for what is true; we long to be who God created us to be. At times our soul is cast down and disquieted within us.[41] That disquiet is our longing for our true selves, in God. Jesus' words continue to speak to us: "Come to me, all you that are weary and are carrying heavy burdens, and I will give you rest. Take my yoke upon you, and learn from me; for I am gentle and humble in heart, and you will find rest for your souls."[42] Learn from one who is gentle and humble in heart. Listen to his voice. Receive from him. And find rest for your soul.

The living Christ continues to speak to us—in our hearts, in nature, through Scripture, within the body of Christ, in acts of justice, with the help of the Spirit, in prayer. Christ's voice can still be heard, if we listen, open and willing to respond, trusting and submitting to that voice. Paul reminds us that "the word is near us, on our lips and in our heart," the word of truth, the word of Christ.[43] We do not run to a set of beliefs, but to Christ, who knows us to the depths of our being. The word that Christ has for us in our present situations is not far away. It is on our lips and in our hearts, as we surrender lips and hearts to God.

We can go to the living Christ, who embodies God's reign, and ask him to reign in our lives. He knows what has usurped his place in our lives. He knows our idols. He knows on what we depend instead of God. He knows the ways of thinking that we devise in order to secure our false allegiances. He knows what we love, serve, go after, and live for. And we can go to him and say, "Lord you know. You know my ways. You know what has me bound. You know what weighs me down. You know my sins. You know where I have wandered away from you. Reign in my heart over the tyrants that have taken hold. Help me to abandon myself completely to you." The good news is that he *does* help us. He helps us do what we have been unable to do.

Then, we, in following Jesus, realize that what we have begun to experience of God's reign is a foretaste of what is to come. We understand that all of human history finds its ultimate goal in Christ, who, as Paul tells us, "hands over the kingdom to God the Father, after he has destroyed every ruler and every authority and power."[44] To this, we are called to be witnesses: we witness before the rulers, governments, and powers of this present age and to those, like us, who hunger and thirst for God. We witness to God's justice, mercy, and faithfulness.

41. Ps 42.
42. Matt 11:28–29.
43. Rom 10:8.
44. 1 Cor 15:24.

Bibliography

Altmann, Walter. *Luther and Liberation: A Latin American Perspective*. Translated by Thea Cooper. 2nd ed. Minneapolis: Fortress, 2015.
Becker, Ernest. *The Denial of Death*. New York: Free Press, 1973.
Bonhoeffer, Dietrich. *Dietrich Bonhoeffer Works, Volume 14: Theological Education at Finkenwalde: 1935–1937*. Edited by H. Galon Barker and Mark S. Brocker. Translated by Douglas W. Stott. Minneapolis: Fortress, 2013.
———. *Dietrich Bonhoeffer Works, Volume 6: Ethics*. Edited by Ilse Tödt et al. Translated by Reinhard Krauss et al. Minneapolis: Fortress, 2009.
———. *A Testament To Freedom: The Essential Writings of Dietrich Bonhoeffer*. Edited by Geffrey B. Kelley and F. Burton Nelson. New York: HarperCollins, 1990.
Cone, James H. *The Cross and the Lynching Tree*. Maryknoll, NY: Orbis, 2011.
Evangelical Lutheran Church in America. *Evangelical Lutheran Worship*. Minneapolis: Fortress, 2006.
Gibson, Jeffery B. *The Disciples' Prayer: The Prayer Jesus Taught in Its Historical Setting*. Minneapolis: Fortress, 2015.
Hauerwas, Stanley. *War and the American Difference: Theological Reflections on Violence and National Identity*. Grand Rapids: Baker Academic, 2011.
Heung-Soo, Kim. "The Korean War (1950–1953) and Christianity: Pro-American Activities of the Christian Churches and the North Korean Reactions." *Madang: Journal of Contextual Theology* 16 (December 2011) 135–158.
Holmes, Barbara A. *Joy Unspeakable: Contemplative Practices of the Black Church*. Minneapolis: Fortress, 2004.
Joseph, Simon J. *The Nonviolent Messiah: Jesus, Q, and the Enochic Tradition*. Minneapolis: Fortress, 2014.
Kierkegaard, Sören. *Purity of Heart is to Will One Thing: A Philosophical Masterpiece*. Jersey City, NJ: Start, 2012. Kindle.
Lizorkin-Eyzenberg, Eliyahu. *The Jewish Gospel of John: Discovering Jesus, King of All Israel*. Jewish Studies for Christians, 2015. Kindle.
McEntee, Rory, and Adam Bucko. *The New Monasticism: An Interspiritual Manifesto for Contemplative Living*. Maryknoll, NY: Orbis, 2015.
Meyers, Robin. *The Underground Church: Reclaiming the subversive way of Jesus*. Londong: SPCK, 2012.
Moltmann, Jürgen. *The Crucified God*. 40th anniversary ed. London: SCM, 2015.
Placher, William C. *Mark*. Belief: A Theological Commentary on the Bible. Louisville: Westminster John Knox, 2010.

Rahner, Karl. *Foundations of Christian Faith: An Introduction to the Idea of Christianity.* Translated by William V. Dych. New York: Seabury, 1978.

Reichelt, Karl Ludvig. *The Transformed Abbott.* London: Lutterworth, 1954.

Sider, Ronald J., ed. *The Early Church on Killing: A Comprehensive Sourcebook on War, Abortion, and Capital Punishment.* Grand Rapids: Baker Academic, 2012.

Thomas, Frank A. *How To Preach A Dangerous Sermon.* Nashville: Abingdon, 2018.

Wallace-Wells, David. *The Uninhabitable Earth: Life After Warming.* New York: Duggan, 2019.

www.ingramcontent.com/pod-product-compliance
Lightning Source LLC
Chambersburg PA
CBHW070926160426
43193CB00011B/1592